PARLIAMENT AND MUMBO-JUMBO

Parliament and Mumbo-Jumbo

BY

EMRYS HUGHES

London
GEORGE ALLEN & UNWIN LTD
RUSKIN HOUSE   MUSEUM STREET

PRINTED IN GREAT BRITAIN
in 11 point Juliana type
BY THE BLACKFRIARS PRESS LTD
LEICESTER

CONTENTS

PREFACE

The purpose of this book is to speed up the process of modernizing Parliament and bringing it up to date so that it can deal more efficiently and speedily with the work of bringing about the social changes in Britain which are so urgent and necessary.

During recent years everyone who has carefully studied parliamentary procedure has realized the importance of Parliament so organizing its work that it earns the respect of people outside and sets an example to other institutions of keeping abreast of the times. The demand for reform has come from many quarters, from within Parliament itself, from the Press, from informed students of politics, who are all anxious that Britain should remain democratic in the fullest sense of the word, especially at a time when the younger and emerging nations of the world are looking to us to give them the benefit of our experience and guidance.

In the Parliament that was elected in 1964 there had been a persistent demand for changes and the parliamentary committees that have been set up have given a great deal of time and thought to the question of how the House of Commons can put its own house in order, and some little concessions have been gained and some slight progress had been made.

But in Parliament itself there is always the dead weight of conservatism and inertia, tradition and resistance to change, and with the struggle of a Labour Government to keep in office with the tiniest majority in recent history the House of Commons has been preoccupied with the day-to-day political struggle and can maintain reasonably that it cannot be expected to do everything that needs to be done at the same time.

So it is all too easy to continue in the old ways and to fall back on the old apologia for doing nothing, or to yield only the slightest concessions so as to give the impression that we are really on the move.

One concedes that the necessary parliamentary reform can only be achieved by a Labour Government with a real working majority, but even then this will not be achieved without persistence and determination from Parliament backed up from outside by a public opinion that realizes what needs to be done and is not afraid of breaks with tradition when these are necessary to maintain really democratic government.

Mr Harold Wilson has spoken out strongly on the need for House of Commons reform.

In a speech at Stowmarket on July 4, 1964, he devoted a great deal of time to advocating parliamentary reform. This was, as far as I can remember, the only occasion in recent years when any leader of a political party devoted a major speech to the subject.

The *Guardian* published its report of Mr Wilson's speech under the headlines

MR WILSON'S PLAN FOR COMMONS REFORM

More Free Votes and All-Party Committees

It said Mr Wilson's speech included proposals for

'Relaxation of the parliamentary voting system to allow more "free votes" and to eliminate the rigid doctrine of each vote involving an issue of confidence.

'Development of all-party committees on the lines of the present Estimates Committee and Public Accounts Committee, not only to make investigations but to draft more controversial legislation.'

Mr Wilson's demand for more 'free votes' was certainly one that should appeal to the backbenchers and help to make Parliament more lively and interesting, although it might mean headaches and nightmares for the Whips on both sides.

Indeed if we are to boast that we have a free Parliament and that we are among the freedom-loving countries, why should there not be more free votes.

In the 1964 Parliament there was a free vote on the abolition of the death penalty for murder.

If M.P.s are to vote as they please on the issue of murder, surely a supremely important issue, why should there not be free votes on other issues and why should the Government not be prepared to accept the decision of the House, which is surely what democracy means?

I read this with more than usual interest (and hope!), for I had been expelled from the Parliamentary Labour Party for voting against the Conservative Government's Air Estimates!

Indeed why should every vote not be a free vote in the real sense of the word, without any coercion on M.P.s by Whips of either side?

I do not mean by this that the Whips should be dispensed with but their function should be guidance, not coercion.

I confess that I have found parliamentary life more interesting and exciting during the occasions when I received no communications from the Whips at all. Not that I was absent from the House, for I voted in the Labour Party lobby more often than the Front Bench. The complaint against me was not that I was not there but that I was there too often.

I am not sure whether it would not be a good thing for any Labour (or Tory) Government to expel about half a dozen of its most independent-minded back benchers after the first Queen's Speech, even although for the purposes of getting unity at a General Election, it would have to re-admit them about a month before the dissolution of Parliament. That would have the inevitable result of keeping any Government on its toes and surely that is what parliamentary democracy is for, isn't it?

When I have seen the Chief Whips on both sides consulting together I am irresistibly reminded of two shepherds discussing the merits of their respective collie dogs at a sheep dog trial.

This speech of Mr Wilson showed quite clearly that he was strongly in favour of parliamentary reforms 'which could go a long way towards restoring to individual back benchers the powers they have been losing to the executive'. Mr Wilson thought that both 'Parliament and public administration could gain from having parliamentary committees under ministerial chairmanship with power to take evidence from experts and outside bodies'. Mr Wilson also argued for an Ombudsman. Indeed his arguments for parliamentary changes were very much the same as those later put before the Select Committee on Procedure by The Study of Parliament Group.

This is exactly the kind of approach to the question of parliamentary reforms that is required and was in striking contrast to the attitude of successive Tory and Labour Leaders of the House.

'Should a drastic reform of Parliament be added to the job list of the next Labour Government?' asked Mr R. H. S. Crossman in an article in the *Guardian* (8.2.63).

'The first task I was given when I entered the Commons in 1945 was to sit on a Select Committee on Procedure, and after that I have never been in any doubt how this question should be answered. More time is wasted and more energy and talent frustrated in the British Parliament than in any other organization of which I have any experience. But alas! Under the Attlee Government and in the first years of Opposition it was difficult to raise the faintest interest either in the National Executive at Transport House or at Westminster for reforms which were dismissed as purely academic.

'Since the 1959 Election, however, the mood has changed. Today a large and influential group of Labour back benchers are ready to consider the case for a radical reform of Parliament itself . . . Their anger is not only prompted by their own personal grievances. Collectively as Members of the House they resent both the rapid decline in its prestige and the process by which it is being stripped of any real rôle in the great decisions of State.'

He concluded:

'I have a hunch that there are a large number of young voters who will be greatly attracted by a political party which frankly admits that the set-up at Westminster is completely out of date and promises to put it right.'

This is the campaign that I am attempting to carry on in this book.

I have of course no right to speak for anybody but myself and in many of the criticisms and suggestions I make, I go a great deal further than many of the advocates of parliamentary reform.

I do not regard myself as anything more than the worker on the factory floor who is invited by the management to put his suggestions for improving the efficiency of the factory in the *Suggestion Box*. I need hardly add that I have not been invited by the management to do this. But I do so, cheerfully, just the same.

EMRYS HUGHES

House of Commons
January 28, 1966

CHAPTER 1

PARLIAMENT RE-BORN

The General Election of October 1964 was a dramatically near thing and there was tense excitement on the day that the results came in and it was impossible to say whether the Labour Party or the Conservative Party had won until the final count showed that there was to be a Labour Government with the tiniest majority in British history.

How could a Government remain in power with a majority over the combined Conservatives and Liberals of only three or four?

So public attention once again turned to the daily proceedings in Parliament with the people of Britain waiting at their television and radio sets late at night to hear if the Labour Government still survived. The people of Britain became interested in what was happening at Westminster once again.

For over a decade the interest in the proceedings of Parliament had steadily declined. There had been successive Conservative Governments for thirteen years and they had comfortable working majorities and were never in danger of defeat. It became generally accepted that to have a Conservative Government was a part of the British way of life.

So the people's interest in what happened from day to day in Parliament steadily waned. They were far more interested in what happened on Saturday at the big football matches. Less and less people came to listen to the debates from the public galleries and the sale of Hansard went steadily down to reach a record low level in the last months of Conservative rule.

With the return of the Labour Government with Harold Wilson as Prime Minister the national interest in politics revived, the galleries became full once more and there were again queues of people waiting to get in, both in St Stephen's Hall and in the streets outside. For a Labour Government again was a novelty and it was anybody's guess as to how long it could last. Parliament had become interesting enough for the big London bookmakers to take a professional interest too and to publish the odds as to how long it would last and what would happen then. If a member of Parliament became ill or had an accident the papers not only published the latest bulletins about his heart condition but his majority at the last election as well.

I shall always remember the day when fog came down over the Glasgow airport on the day when the Government was faced with a vote of censure and when eight Scottish Members of Parliament were held up for a few hours until a plane could take us from Prestwick. We became conscious of the fact that we were of national importance when the newspaper reporters and the television camera men arrived at the air terminal in Renfrew. All this had happened before but this was the first time we had been given the treatment of film stars and celebrities. The press men explained that they had been phoned up from their London offices, the camera men explained that our photographs were needed for the BBC and ITV news bulletins. The whole future of the country depended on whether we arrived in London in time for the vote. We were taken by bus from Renfrew to Prestwick through the fog and the reporters and the camera men were waiting for us again and when the plane arrived at London Airport the television cameras were whining as we went down the gangway while the reporters were waiting on the tarmac to tell us that we were front page headlines in the evening papers and what were our comments? Never had we arrived in London in such a blaze of publicity. Even the *Daily Telegraph* published our photographs on the front page next day and our arrival appeared on the TV screens all over the country so that our constituents knew that their Members had arrived. Without any effort on our part we had been given enormous publicity and were regarded as the central figures of a major political drama, for with our arrival the Government was saved and no General Election was imminent.

And, at the House of Commons, we had a reception of a kind we had never had before and which we could hardly hope for again. The Whips shook us warmly by the hand and even the most serious of them all, the Scottish Whip, Mr. George Lawson, who during the time I had been expelled from the Parliamentary Labour Party in the days of the previous Government was inclined to look upon me as Enemy Number One, positively beamed on me.

That incident showed how important M.P.s had become. We became intensely aware that the people of Britain had become more interested in Parliament and what happened there than they had been for a long time. This had come as a result of the narrow Government majority which might disappear overnight and the struggle of the Wilson Government to keep going, and curiosity on the part of the people as to what might happen if a General Election came suddenly again and the effect this might have on their lives. So with every day and every issue that arose containing the possibility of dramatic developments, more attention was directed to Westminster and what was going on there. When two M.P.s, Woodrow Wyatt and Desmond Donnelly, threatened either to vote against the White Paper on Steel or to abstain in the division and threatened to bring down the Government light was thrown on the way M.P.s voted, and whether, in view of the fact that they had supported a party that had pledged itself to the nationalisation of steel in its election manifesto, they should be allowed to remain in the Labour Party. Party discipline, which had hitherto been a matter of little concern outside political circles, became a matter of interest to the man in the street. Then when it was reported that when a vital division took place, sick M.P.s had to be brought to the precincts of Westminster from hospitals in ambulances, the question was naturally asked whether this was an intelligent or humane way of carrying on national business. People in the morning listening to the seven or eight o'clock news bulletins on the radio and hearing that the House of Commons was still sitting began to wonder too. Then there was the occasion when in the early hours one morning the Government was defeated because a number of Opposition M.P.s whom the Government Whips thought were peacefully slumbering in their beds suddenly arrived, and the episode when the voting being equal the Conservative Chairman of the Committee acted strictly according to precedent and gave his casting vote to the Government.

The day-to-day procedure of Parliament, the pairing arrangements between M.P.s, the Whips and their functions, the question of whether it wouldn't be more sensible for Parliament to meet in the mornings or for the Finance Bill to be sent to Committee instead of taking up weeks of discussion on the floor of the House resulted in the inevitable questions, 'Does not Parliament need to be reformed?', 'Why should the House of Commons continue to be run as it was in the last century?'

At the General Election there had been a great deal of discussion by all parties of the need for modernization of British industry. No wonder people outside began to ask 'Isn't it time that Parliament modernized itself?'

Then there was another factor that made for change. At the General Election of 1964 a considerable number of new M.P.s had arrived. Many of them, especially on the Government side, were young and critical and energetic and were not at all satisfied at being regarded as sheep to be shepherded into the division lobbies. Many of them had a suspicion before they arrived that changes were necessary and that Parliamentary machinery needed to be speeded up.

But when they were faced with the day-to-day routine in Parliament they naturally exclaimed 'Good God, what is all this?'

I was delighted to hear them ask this question for I had been asking it without getting any very satisfactory answer for nearly twenty years.

I cannot say whether any of the young Tories who first arrived at the elections felt this way too. Perhaps they did, though so many of them were educated at the public schools that they find difficulty in getting out of their heads all the stuff from the history books that has led them to think that the British House of Commons is one of those ancient and venerable institutions that must not be changed but accepted like 'Rule Britannia' and the playing fields of Eton and all the rest of it.

But the Socialists should take a different view of things. They were sent to Parliament to establish a different kind of society and the House of Commons should be the place in which to get things done.

Drastic changes in Parliament could not be achieved when a Labour Government with a majority of three literally hung on by its teeth and had to deal with baffling and difficult economic problems. The time, however, cannot long be delayed before Parliament is forced by events or from the outside. We cannot go through a time of great economic changes without adapting our political institutions to new conditions and perhaps some of the challenges I throw out in this book will not go unnoticed.

CHAPTER 2

THE WESTMINSTER MUSEUM

Aneurin Bevan once remarked that the new M.P. was subdued by the fact that Westminster had the appearance and the atmosphere of a church. There is something in this for the Central Lobby with its high dome and mosaics and candelabra and arches is reminiscent of Notre Dame or Cologne Cathedral. But there it ends. To me the Palace of Westminster is a huge, rambling, badly laid out museum.

Indeed that is how it is regarded by visitors, especially those who come from overseas. In summer and holiday times thousands of people are shepherded through it every week by Members and by guides. It is one of the sights of London which must be seen like Buckingham Palace, the Tower of London, the Zoo and Madame Tussauds.

Whenever I see these hordes of schoolchildren being led along the corridors by M.P.s who think it is their duty to their constituents and perhaps with an idea at the back of their heads that the teachers and the children will report back home what a nice obliging man their Member of Parliament is and that there is a chance of picking up a few votes as a result of their labours I cannot help feeling that the National Society for the Prevention of Cruelty to Children should really do something about it.

There is a lot to be said for keeping organized parties of children of sixteen out of the place altogether. Every time I see these classes of children bored to death after the first five minutes I feel a deep sense of gratitude that South Ayrshire is so far away from London and the cost of bringing the children there prohibitive. And I am quite sure that London and South of England M.P.s would cordially agree with me although they might not consider it advisable to say so. Westminster is not for young children so why bore them by trailing them along its corridors when they would be far happier and learn more at the Zoo.

Nobody can however completely escape from showing visitors

around the House of Commons but they should be old enough to take things in and understand.

One of my duties for many years has been to take a party of boys and girls from West Berlin around the Palace of Westminster. I met the schoolmaster in Berlin just after the war and their visit, on their way to a school in the North of England, has been an annual event ever since. They want to know everything, these young Germans, and the questioning begins as soon as you meet them at the Norman Gate at the entrance to the House of Lords. They have already questioned their teachers about the statue of Richard Coeur de Lion on horseback and who he was and what he did. I once rescued a party of Russians from a guide there who had been explaining to them that King Richard was there because he had been to Palestine fighting the Jews. The Russians were puzzled because they had not realized that Fascist anti-Semitism in Britain went so far back.

There is a big oil painting of Queen Victoria in all her glory at the top of the staircase leading to the House of Lords and the young Germans always stop to pay their respects to her. Of course they all know that Queen Victoria was a German and that she married a German prince, and reason from this that our Royal Family are Germans. Wasn't she the grandmother of the Kaiser? One of the more persistent boys points out that the Kaiser must have been our Queen's grand uncle and from then on whenever they see a portrait of a King or Queen they trace the relationship to Queen Victoria and Prince Albert. They take a proprietary interest in all the portraits of the Georges on the walls of the Royal Gallery and are quite proud of the fact that they were exports from Germany.

In the Queen's Robing Room with its small throne I explain that this is where the Queen comes first when she comes to Parliament to deliver the Queen's Speech. 'Is it her own speech?' 'Does she decide what she is to speak about?' 'Why isn't she allowed to make her own speech?' I tell them that the Queen's Speech isn't really the Queen's Speech but the Government's programme of what it intends doing in the session of Parliament that is about to commence and that the Queen is not consulted about it, but just reads it out whether she agrees with what is in it or not. It takes a lot to convince them that the Queen does not take a prominent part in the Government of Britain and does not matter a great deal in British politics. Constitutional monarchy is not something that is quickly explained to people from other countries and they look rather disappointed about it. Somebody invariably asks 'If the Queen hasn't much power why do you need to pay her so much money?' I politely ignore the question and direct their attention to the big wall paintings of the Battles of Trafalgar and Waterloo. They are not much interested in Trafalgar but they know all about Waterloo. When they see the picture of Wellington shaking hands with Blucher after the battle, that confirms their theories that Waterloo was a great victory for the Germans and that this is proved by Wellington shaking hands with him and congratulating him on it. Different nationalities draw different deductions from it. A group of Russian students thought that the credit for Waterloo and the bringing down of Napoleon belonged neither to Wellington nor Blucher. They had been in that war too and Napoleon's final defeat had only been possible because the Russians had destroyed so many of his best regiments in the retreat from Moscow, and history had repeated itself in World War Two when they had destroyed the armies of Hitler. You see history in different lights according to the nationality of the visitors you take through the Royal Gallery. As for the French, well, you politely hurry through.

But before I leave the Royal Gallery let me stop to throw out a suggestion. If children are to be brought to Westminster to learn their history why not turn the Royal Gallery into a historical museum, with models and pictures and manuscripts showing what the real history of the country has been like. It is a spacious hall with plenty of floor space and if those huge portraits of kings and queens and their relatives were reduced in size with many of them, including those vast portrayals in ghastly detail of the Battles of Trafalgar and Waterloo, removed to the Chamber of Horrors at Madame Tussauds, a real good job could be made of it and the visits to Westminster made worthwhile.

From the Royal Gallery we make our way into the ante room to the House of Lords and there the German students hail with delight the sight of the paintings of Henry the Eighth and his wives. They have all heard of him. Of all the kings and queens of England, the long lists of Edwards and Henrys, it is the eighth

Henry that seems to have got his place in the textbooks of the nations of the world. It is not the Reformation and the part that Henry's matrimonial problems played in precipitating that religious revolution that has got him into the headlines of history, but the way he had of disposing of his wives. They stop longer in fascination over Henry than they do before all the Georges in the Royal Gallery put together. Which of the wives were beheaded and why? One feels that of all the memories they take away with them from the Museum of Westminster the most vivid is that of Henry the Eighth and the unfortunate ladies whose portraits are beside him in the ante room to the House of Lords.

As soon as we enter the House of Lords and they see the throne the questions return to the Queen's Speech. 'When the Queen delivers the speech from the throne does she do it standing up or sitting down and why?' 'And why isn't there a throne for the Queen's husband and what does he do when she is reading her speech?' Questions come like a burst of firing from machine guns in the House of Lords which with the throne and the woolsack, and the red leather benches with the microphones fitted into the backs, is the spectacle of the place. They have been told all about the Woolsack and have heard that it is stuffed with horse hair and not wool. 'Why?' 'Do the Lords always wear their robes and why not?' 'Is it because they are all so old and deaf that they need the microphones at the backs of their seats?' A young girl is curious whether there are many lady lords and whether they too wear robes—and hats. They have heard about life peers and the peers who have inherited their titles. 'How many come?' 'Are they paid?' 'What power has the House of Lords over what the House of Commons does?' 'If it hasn't much why isn't it abolished?' 'Isn't it very expensive to keep it lighted and heated and cleaned if they do so little work?' 'Why do we still allow the bishops of the Church of England to sit in the House of Lords and keep the Roman Catholic bishops out?'

Their thirst for information about the House of Lords is hard to quench, although one has the feeling that they know most of the answers already and only want to air their knowledge or have their suspicions confirmed.

When we leave the House of Lords I feel that the back of the job is broken. The paintings on the walls of the corridor going into the Central Lobby are about Parliament's struggles with the King and the Civil War, and although they know all about the execution of Charles the First they want to know all about it again. It is when we reach the corner lobby of the House of Commons that I feel I am entitled to get a little of my own back and explain that we had to build a new House of Commons because the old one was destroyed when the German planes bombed London in the last war. I do this rather guiltily because these young Germans were not born then. But a little reminder now and then, especially to the new generation growing up in Berlin, many of whom seem to think that history began when the Russians invaded Germany without provocation in 1945.

In the House of Commons they all want to know the place where Churchill sat. Why they should regard him as one of their national heroes I do not know. They make to sit down on the sacred spot but the policeman on duty knows all about this and stops them in time.

The House of Commons does not usually interest them as much as the House of Lords—and the questions get less from exhaustion. 'Where does the Prime Minister sit?' 'Why does the Speaker need to wear a wig?' 'What is in the dispatch boxes?' 'What do they put into that big purse that hangs behind the Speaker's chair?' 'Why is the place so small?' 'Why isn't there a seat for every Member?' 'How does the Speaker know who to call on to speak?'

On the whole I think it is not unfair to say that these German schoolboys and schoolgirls get their money's worth. I have not disclosed the answers I gave to their questions. Perhaps that will come later in this book. In any case I will not disclose my hand in advance because another lot will probably arrive next year.

After we have adjourned to the Terrace for the purpose of giving them a further opportunity of asking the questions they may have forgotten, I ask them some questions in return. And I learn a lot from them.

I wonder what impression is left on their minds about the Palace of Westminster, the British Parliament and what they have seen there. They are very polite and grateful to me but what will they remember about it? Do they go back to Berlin impressed with the way we do our business and how efficiently

British democracy sets an example to them and to the world? Or do they think that they have seen one of the sights of London and have been as interested in it as if they had been shown around some antiquarian museum or some old curiosity shop?

CHAPTER 3

'FE-FI-FO-FUM'

The Speaker's Procession is a sight that M.P.s tell their visitors they simply must see. I have even heard it described as one of the sights that brings foreigners to London and helps the tourist trade. Every afternoon at two-thirty on weekdays and at eleven o'clock on Fridays, when the House meets in the mornings, the strangers in the Central Lobby are warned that they must expect some solemn event and the police make a passage through the assembled people so that the Procession may pass. A hushed silence descends on the Lobby. There is a story told of an occasion when Neil Maclean, the veteran Clydeside M.P., had brought some Glasgow visitors to see the fun.

Before the police inspector could remove his helmet and shout out the traditional cry of 'Hats Off, Strangers' another Glasgow visitor on the other side of the Lobby recognized Maclean and in his enthusiasm shouted 'Neil'. Promptly several strangers went down on their knees.

One can hear the measured tread of the feet on the stone floor of the corridor before they come into view. One, two, three, four, or as one irreverent M.P. used to whisper, 'Fee, fi, fo, fum'.

Heading the procession comes an attendant dressed like a waiter, with knee breeches, black stockings and bright buckled shoes, carrying white gloves, stepping out like a guardsman on parade. Behind him comes the Sergeant-at-Arms carrying the gold mace, then the Speaker in black robes, black silk stockings, etc., with his face partially hidden by a big white wig. Then comes the trainbearer and finally the Chaplain who is to read the prayers in his clerical robes and the Speaker's Secretary in a black frock coat. Every face is serious and solemn and it reminds one of the procession that accompanies a condemned man to the scaffold. They make a right-angled turn in the middle of the Lobby and the sound of their tread can be heard as they go along the corridor into the Members' Lobby where the police, helmets off, and the attendants stand at attention and into the

Chamber, and the doors close behind them.

I do not know how long the procession has been going on but it is probably of religious origin with the Mace, the symbol of the authority of the Crown, taking the place of the Cross. It is supposed to impress the strangers in the Lobby with the dignity and authority of the Speaker and the solemnity and sanctity of the place. The House of Lords has a somewhat similar Procession with the Lord Chancellor instead of the Speaker. There have been three Speakers in my time. The first, Colonel Clifton Browne, was an old army officer and carried himself as if he were on a military parade, and I rather felt this kind of uniform out of place. W. S. Morrison was a tall, rugged, handsome Scottish Highlander who was a superb actor and for the occasion put on an expression of gravity and melancholy as if he were being led to execution himself. 'Shakes' Morrison missed a magnificent opportunity to make the procession really impressive and colourful. He could have appeared in his native kilt. The last Speaker, Sir Harry Hilton Foster, looked straight in front of him with an air of determination as if he were going to read the Riot Act at Trafalgar Square.

Undoubtedly Queen Anne or Queen Victoria would thoroughly have approved of it and so perhaps might Sir Laurence Olivier and Sir John Gielgud, although they might improve it a bit. But are we in the twentieth century or are we at some performance at the Old Vic?

Is this journey necessary in these days? I feel certain that the audiences for which it is staged are not so impressed as we think they are. The visitors from Central Africa might approve with reservations that it could do with some of their more flamboyant colours in the costumes. But Europeans and Americans look respectfully puzzled that such customs and costumes and rituals still survive in the Britain of today. They may be too polite to say so but there is the shrug of the shoulders and the sympathetic smile.[1]

Most of us know the old story that the Chaplain looks at the Members and prays for the country. There are not, however, many Members to look at. Churchgoing has greatly declined since the war and this applies to the House of Commons. There is nothing more mechanical than the prayers there. The number

[1] For the official account of the proceedings see Appendix 1.

of M.P.s that attend for devotional purposes is a mere handful,
I nearly wrote 'almost nil'. One cannot expect the Noncon-
formists, the Roman Catholics, the Jews, the Scots and the
agnostics to take much interest in it, for they are not Church of
England anyway and the C. of E. has the monopoly of the
Palace of Westminster because it is the established ceremonial
religion and for ecclesiastical purposes it comes under the
authority of the Dean of Westminster. The Members who are
there are those who want to make sure of their seats for the
subsequent proceedings, those who have the first questions,
or those who are waiting their chance to get tickets for the
gallery from the Sergeant-at-Arms as soon as the praying is over.
Both the first Benches are usually empty. I never remember
seeing Sir Winston Churchill in for prayers, nor any subsequent
Prime Minister or Leader of the Opposition. I have heard that
Mr. Gladstone was the last Prime Minister to turn up regularly
at prayers. The public and the press galleries are empty for they
are not allowed in, although why the press should not be prayed
for I do not know. Surely they need it as much as anybody else!
The Speaker does not go to the chair but with the Chaplain
kneels at the Table during the recital of the prayers from the
Prayer Book, and when it comes to the Lord's Prayer the Members turn round and face the walls, a custom which dates from
the time when Members thought they should kneel. Meanwhile
the attendants at the glass doors wait for the signal that it is all
over, occasionally calling for silence from the Members who
have begun to arrive and are waiting to get in for question time.

Only on Budget Days are the benches full, and that is because
they want to get their seats. Prayers are a part of the ritual of
the place and I doubt whether even the most devout of the
Members get an emotional kick out of it after they have been
there once or twice. I once remarked in a debate on the Air
Forces Estimates that religion was in order for the first five minutes
of the day's proceedings and out of order for the rest of the day.
Nobody thinks that prayers matter much. When somebody once
suggested that perhaps it would be more appropriate if prayers
were offered at the end of the day he was reminded that this
was not fair to the Chaplain because then he would have nobody
to pray for.

Prayers are part of the ritual of the place, like many of the

other proceedings at Westminster. There may be no particular
reason nowadays for this custom or for that except that this was
done yesterday or the day before.

The Chaplain for example always leaves the Chamber walk-
ing backwards as far as the bar, and so is sometimes in danger
of colliding with Members who come hurrying in. But the
Sergeant-at-Arms, when he goes to the Table to remove the
mace from the Table, does not have to perform the feat of walk-
ing backwards, but the Comptroller of the Household (one of
the Whips), who comes with a message from the Queen, has to
walk backwards after he has done his job, and he must give a
sigh of relief when he arrives safely at the bar and is able to
safely retire to get rid of his billiard cue and his frock coat.

Why he should not be allowed to turn and walk out normally
after he has finished his job (an unnecessary one anyway, the
communication could be read by the Clerk) nobody can reasonably explain. If the attendants who carry in the bundles of petitions that are periodically presented by Members are not condemned to walk backwards after they have done their job why
should anybody else?

All this slow motion march takes place every day before the
House is at last able to begin its work and before the honourable
Member for —— who has been carefully rehearsing in his mind,
during the prayers of the Chaplain, his supplementary to his
question demanding to know why the Minister of Technology
is not doing more to speed up modern methods in British industry, can at last say 'Mr Speaker, Number 1'.

Let me hasten to explain. I am not asking for the exclusion of
religion from the Palace of Westminster. Prayers, for those who
wished to hear them, could be held in the Crypt of Edward the
Confessor, which is traditionally the right place.

The Sergeant-at-Arms or his deputies sit on a raised chair
during the sittings of the House and remove the mace without
any ceremony when the House rises. When the House goes into
Committee he removes the mace from the Table on to a bracket
and when the Committee stage is over he places it on the Table
again, and quite a lot of this goes on. There is no real reason for
this except tradition, for every Member must know when the
Speaker or the Deputy Speaker is in the chair and that when
the Chairman of Committees or one of his deputies is sitting at

the Table that it is the Committee stage of a bill. Any M.P. who only realizes that the House is in Committee when the mace is not *on* the table ought not to be there.

The Sergeant-at-Arms is also supposed to go into action if a Member is suspended, but that is not why he wears a sword. If he drew his sword and impaled a Member he would find himself not at Westminster but at the Old Bailey. There has been only one suspension for refusing to obey the chair during the last twenty years so the duties of the Sergeant-at-Arms as Chief Chucker Out are not onerous. Another of his duties is to hand out gallery tickets to Members who want to get visitors into the gallery when the House is sitting. This could easily be done by an attendant in the Lobby or by an automatic machine. I do not know what useful purpose is served by having the Sergeant-at-Arms in the Chamber during the sittings of the House or why he should have to be bored in this way.

Outside the Chamber he is the business manager of the House of Commons and is the head of the staff that runs the place. But he is not appointed by the House but by the Queen, for Westminster is a Royal Palace. The present Sergeant-at-Arms is an ex-admiral and his predecessor was an ex-general. Ex high ranking officers from the navy and the army were appointed alternatively but recently it was conveyed to the Queen that in future the House should be consulted and in future this is to be done.

The House of Commons is neither an army nor a ship and there is no real reason why the job should not be advertised and the most capable applicant appointed.

The House of Lords has its own Sergeant-at-Arms, called Black Rod, who has a very similar uniform and who appears at the House of Commons, sometimes at inappropriate times, to summon M.P.s to the House of Lords to hear the Royal Assent given to bills. The door is shut in his face and he has to knock three times (this dates from the time of the differences between the Commons and the King), and then the Members led by the Speaker go off to the Lords. This procedure is now generally recognized as a nuisance and a waste of time and in the debate on the Consolidation Bill in July of last year some M.P.s led by Sir Geoffrey de Freitas continued the debate, and as he is an ex-Colonial Governor and so by no means on the Left but is usually on the side of the Establishment it will be seen that the

arrival of Black Rod, when M.P.s are anxious to discuss something more important, is not an event that is greeted with overwhelming enthusiasm.

Now I am not by temperament a discourteous person but if
this ancient and honourable custom continues and M.P.s find
their debates being interrupted by somebody who has had the
door locked against him purposely for the occasion, somebody
might move that he can knock and knock and knock again and
so a new precedent be created, which would be that the House
of Commons considers that it is quite undignified for the elected
representatives of the nation to be lined up and shepherded off
to the House of Lords to be informed that Her Majesty has been
graciously pleased to give her assent to legislation which she has
to assent to anyway. And this inevitably leads me to a discussion
of what should be the relationship between the House of
Commons and the Crown in these democratic days.

CHAPTER 4

PARLIAMENT AND THE CROWN

Ought we to scrap monarchy like almost every civilized government in the world has done and go in for a democratically
elected President?

In theory I would say emphatically 'Yes'. There is not the
slightest justification for a hereditary monarchy these days any
more than there is for hereditary lords, or hereditary M.P.s or
hereditary Prime Ministers. Much as Sir Winston Churchill
came to be regarded in his lifetime as a national spokesman even
Sir Alec Douglas Home or Lord Salisbury or any of the extreme
Right of the Conservative Party would have been prepared to
lead a Revolution if it had been proposed that he should have
been succeeded as Prime Minister by his son Mr Randolph
Churchill.

Even the most conservative vicar who has broken off relations
with his bishop and emptied his church of his congregation
except the verger by his paleolithic sermons would not insult
the intelligence nor test the loyalty of that gentleman by preach-
ing a sermon advocating that the Archbishop of Canterbury
should be succeeded as head of the Church of England by his
eldest daughter.

But illogical as the position of the monarchy is in the twentieth century there is far less republicanism in the country today
than there was in the time when Mr. Joseph Chamberlain was
one of its advocates. Not even the Communist Party puts the
abolition of the monarchy in its election programme and if a
resolution proposing it appeared on the list of resolutions appearing on the annual agenda of the Labour Party Conference everyone would suspect that the constituency party that proposed it
had been permeated by the Conservatives or the anarchists for
the purpose of bringing about the downfall of the Labour Party
at the next election.

It is not that the British people are so enthusiastic about the
monarchy as they are supposed to be but because they cannot

yet bring themselves to think of anything else. The Conservative Party, who have always wrapped themselves round with the Union Jack at election times and pose as the great super patriotic party in order to get power in order that they can rob and exploit the majority in the interests of the few, are of course in favour of the monarchy to the last man, woman and child. And as the purpose of the Labour Party is to change the economic system of society in order to prevent the nation being robbed and exploited by the super patriots, republicanism is not in its list of priorities nor does it want any chasing after red herrings even if they are dressed up in red, white and blue. So Mr Harold Wilson dutifully departs to Buckingham Palace and Balmoral, as he goes off to read the lessons at Westminster Abbey or at some Methodist church in Blackpool or Brighton on the Sunday of the Labour Party Conference, realising that on these occasions he must prove himself to be the most devout and conventional conformist. Nowadays the most extreme Left Winger on the Labour benches would no more dream of putting down a motion for the abolition of the monarchy than he would dream of tabling one in favour of the abolition of Bertram Mills' circus.

Those of us who moved the reduction of sums voted for their lifetime to the Queen and the Duke of Edinburgh and the rest of the Royal Family on the occasion of the Civil List, proposed when Queen Elizabeth the Second came to the throne, did so for the same reasons that Mr Iain Macleod advocated the reduction of taxation (not specifying where the reduction would be effected), so as to ease the burdens of the hard-pressed British taxpayer. Our case was not that the monarchy should be abolished on that occasion but that it could be run more cheaply and less extravagantly. This the British taxpayer can understand. If a Gallup Poll were carried out tomorrow as to whether the monarchy should be abolished the vote against would no doubt be overwhelming. But if there were to be a referendum as to whether the super expensive Royal Yacht *Britannia*, which was camouflaged as a hospital ship in the 1951 Re-armament Programme to get it through an unsuspecting House of Commons, should be allocated to the Ministry of Health for giving voyages to old age pensioners or the disabled the result might be rather different.

When I have taken a critical line on the unnecessary expenditure on the Royal Yacht and similar occasions I have been surprised to find by my correspondence that I had taken a line which was far more popular outside than inside the House of Commons, which on such matters is sickeningly sychophantic and servile.

But the fact that there is no immediate demand for old-fashioned republicanism and will probably never be unless Royalty obtrudes itself unnecessarily into political controversy, does not mean that a House of Commons that wants to modernize its procedure should not direct its mind to considering whether all this make-believe and traditional ritual that the Queen is some superior being in the background, is necessary nor that the time has not definitely come for a lot of these time-wasting conventions to be discreetly dropped.

Walter Bagelot in his classical book *The English Constitution* has laid it down that the Queen must give her assent to legislation passed by Parliament whether she approves of it or not, even if it meant signing her own death warrant.

Yet every Bill that is presented to Parliament has to begin with the ancient phraseology:

'Be it enacted by the Queen's most Excellent Majesty, by and with the advice and consent of the Lords Spiritual and Temporal, and Commons, in this present Parliament assembled, and by the authority of this same as follows.'

Of course the Queen has to sign on the dotted line whether she likes it or not. So why go on repeating the incantations that mean nothing.

Indeed why should the Queen be asked to sign anything at all? A person's signature is meaningless if the person has no earthly idea of what it is all about. Nobody can possibly read or understand what the Queen has to give her assent to in every Parliamentary session. Nobody, for example, except a highly qualified and experienced chartered accountant could possibly understand all the clauses, sub-sections and schedules of the last controversial Finance Bill. Why then should the Queen be compelled to write out her signature so many hundreds of times a year as if she were a schoolgirl writing out her name so many times for some misconduct in the classroom?

One would think that a great sigh of relief would go up from Buckingham Palace if it were politely conveyed to Her Majesty that in future all these documents would be signed by the Speaker. I am aware of course that the ultra constitutionalists and the monarchists will perhaps faint at this suggestion and remonstrate that I am taking away the powers of the Queen, interfering with the Royal Prerogative, and that I am attempting to establish a republic by stealth. Yet they must admit that the Queen's signature is only a formality and really an unnecessary formality.

When the Speaker gives his decision that a bill is a money bill, then the House of Lords cannot interfere with it. So the precedent of the Speaker's signature has already been established. The Speaker could do all the signing that is necessary and he, of course, has or should have an idea of what it is all about. Thus, the trailing away of the House of Commons to the House of Lords and the holding up of business, and all the hat raising and bowing in the Lords as if we were in a Christmas pantomime, would be abolished. Of course visitors to the House of Lords galleries on such occasions are interested in these proceedings, which are more colourful than the debates, but does Parliament exist for the purpose of providing visitors in the galleries with free pantomimes?

In spite of all this hocus pocus that the Queen is really interested in what goes on in the House of Commons, in practice the Queen is prevented from ever going to the place to see what is going on there. Television is her only hope. If the Queen arrived incognito in the Lobby of the House of Commons and got past the police who failed to recognize her, sent a green card for a Member and thus succeeded in getting into the Public Gallery, it would be the duty of the attendants to show her out.

This tradition dates back to the time when the House of Commons objected to the habit of Charles I arriving at Westminster with his soldiers to arrest the Members. So nowadays the reigning monarch is the one British citizen who is barred from seeing and hearing what goes on in the House of Commons and listening to the explanations and debates about the legislation that she is supposed to approve.

She has thus less privileges than the wife of the Speaker, who has a special seat.

C

Then comes the question of the Queen's Speech. The German schoolboys were genuinely perplexed as to why the Queen makes the speech and who makes it for her and why. We might very well ask the same questions. The Queen has no more to do with what is in the speech than the inspector of the Westminster police or the Sergeant-at-Arms. She has just to read out the document that the Prime Minister and the Cabinet has asked her to read. It is usually the most controversial document of the Parliamentary session and frequently leads to embittered and acrimonious debates. But nobody blames the Queen for it. The Queen was not attacked because she announced the intention of the Government to introduce the nationalization of iron and steel.

M.P.s who do not want to hear the Queen reading somebody else's speech and to study what is in it without having their attention distracted by the sight of the peeresses in their robes and all the gilt and ceremony can get the printed speech from the Vote Office almost as soon as the Queen has finished it. Besides, if they have poor eyesight, that is provided for too. For it is the custom for the Speaker to read out the speech again in spite of the fact that M.P.s who have gone to the Lords have already heard it once and have the printed copy in front of them.

When the debates on the Address are over the Queen gets a letter of thanks from the House of Commons for the speech she hasn't written and throughout the debate the pretence is carried on that she has had something to do with it.

Why should the Queen be brought into all this business of the Government's programme and Parliamentary discussion of it at all? The traditionalists will say that the public outside enjoy the sight of the horses and the colour of the uniforms as the Royal Procession proceeds from Buckingham Palace to Westminster. This of course is the case for the free spectacle and the free pantomime. Bread and circuses have from Roman times been the motto of the establishment throughout the ages. The case for the monarchy getting mixed up with modern government is that an elected president might more easily become a dictator than a monarch and that the monarchy is purely decorative and a harmless anachronism anyway, provided it does not interfere with, or obtrude itself, on Parliament and doesn't interfere with or clutter up the traffic which can also be an important consideration for the police trying to control it on State occasions.

If Queen Elizabeth the Second lives as long as Queen Victoria, according to precedent—and the expectation of life has increased during this century—she might live to be the first British monarch to become a centenarian, if she hasn't become so bored with the whole business long before then and decided like Queen Wilhelmina, that she should join the old age pensioners and abdicate. One cannot prophesy what the public mood will be like in the year 2000 or whether the artists who are designing the postage stamps will be still struggling with how to commemorate some birthday or important event and squeeze the Queen's head in at the same time. The Queen's head is getting smaller and smaller on the postage stamps. The part that the monarchy plays, or is supposed to play, in government will get less too if Parliament has made up its mind that it has so many things that are important to do and that it should dispense with the flummery and get on with the job.

I am, of course, only writing about mumbo-jumbo as it affects Parliament, not how it operates outside. I do not suggest retiring the Queen or making the rest of the Royal Family redundant. Anything I have suggested would not interfere with the Queen's position as the ceremonial head of state, or visiting the Commonwealth and foreign countries as such, or in receiving diplomats, entertaining heads of state and continuing the other conventional duties of the monarch.

What I want to do is to relieve Her Majesty and Parliament of all this time-wasting, ancient routine based on the fiction that in these days real power rests with the monarchy. It doesn't. The Duke of Windsor can completely endorse this. Popular as Edward VIII was, he was left with no delusions that he could overrule the Prime Minister and Parliament, and even all the rhetoric of Winston Churchill could not save him. Why should Queen Elizabeth be shut up in her room eternally signing documents in which she cannot possibly be interested and carry on with all the ritual which had to be gone through by Queen Elizabeth the First, Queen Anne and Queen Victoria? There is no more reason why she should have to do what Queen Victoria did any more than she should wear Queen Victoria's old clothes.

Of course the relations between the monarchy and Parliament have changed a great deal in this century. That is quite clear to anyone who reads the Duke of Windsor's revealing autobiography and Professor John P. Mackintosh's intensely interesting classic *The British Cabinet.*

King Edward could write to Mr Balfour in 1902 about a proposed reshuffle of the Cabinet: 'With regard to appointments I conclude they will naturally not be offered until after full consultation with me'. One cannot imagine the present Queen writing to either Mr Macmillan, Sir Alec Douglas Home or Mr Harold Wilson in this strain.

If King George VI had written to Clem Attlee protesting about Aneurin Bevan's speeches and demanding an explanation (as King Edward did to Asquith about Lloyd George's famous anti-landlord Limehouse speech), Attlee would probably have replied in one of his laconic notes 'This has nothing to do with you'.

Professor Mackintosh tells us that 'only once after 1922 is there any record of the King's views being mentioned in the Cabinet. When King George remonstrated with Arthur Henderson about the Labour Government's decision to recognize Russia and receive an ambassador from the régime which had murdered his cousins, The Tsar, the Tsarina and their children, Henderson reported: 'I didn't argue or interrupt. I just let him run on. And then I said "Well, Your Majesty, that's the Cabinet decision to exchange Ambassadors but perhaps the Prince of Wales could do it for you" and the Russian Ambassador was received.'

King Edward VIII had no opportunities to interfere with Parliament, his reign was too short. His grievance was that Parliament disastrously interfered with him.

George VI made one or two feeble attempts to assert the authority that he really hadn't got. He was a supporter of Neville Chamberlain and did not want Churchill. He thought Chamberlain was being stabbed 'in the back from both sides' (a rather difficult operation).

'When the war was over,' writes Professor Mackintosh, 'the Labour Government never experienced any difficulty with King

George though he had no understanding of its aims . . . Yet
there can be no doubt that the King felt a certain relief when
that party returned in 1951.'

'King George VI', is the summing up, 'had virtually no
impact on public policy.'

From all that we can gather King George VI was a pains-
taking and conscientious public servant who took his duties very
seriously and these wore him down. How many documents,
which he could not possibly understand, were presented him for
his signature during his comparatively short reign one cannot
say, but they must have been enormous. Why should we inflict
these unnecessary duties on a suffering sovereign?

So let us say 'God Save the Queen' from ancient routine
formalities. At the same time let us remember the verses of
Robert Burns which ended with the refrain

> 'And when we sing "God Save the King"
> We'll ne'er forget the people.'

and say God save the poor old Mother of Parliaments from
wasting time on doing things, just because we have been doing
them for hundreds of years and which have no relevance to the
world of today, for there is no need to waste her time either for
she is very busy and has a lot of work to do.

We should modernize the monarchy and modernize Parliament at the same time.

CHAPTER 5

THE HOUSE OF LORDS—END IT OR MEND IT?

'A state of gradual decline was what the average Englishman has come to associate with the House of Lords. Little by little, we might have expected, it would have ceased to take a controversial part in practical politics. Year by year, it would have faded more completely into the past to which it belongs until, like Jack-in-the-Green or Punch and Judy, only a picturesque and fitfully lingering memory would have remained.'

So said Winston Churchill, when as a Minister in a Liberal Government he was stumping the country in 1908, denouncing the House of Lords.

It was to Churchill's credit that he steadfastly refused to go to the House of Lords when he gave up the Prime Ministership and remained in the House of Commons until almost the end of his life.

But the House of Lords remains, half a century after Churchill made this speech prophesying its demise.

True the great controversy of 1908 to 1910 resulted in the powers of the House being curtailed. It ended the Lords powers over finance and the legislation passed in the Labour Government of 1951 reduced the time it could delay legislation to a few months.

What is going to happen to the House of Lords next?

In recent years we have had the legislation creating the new kind of peers—the life peers, and ladies are now in the House of Lords and an attempt is made to portray it as the House of the Elder Statesmen, the really wise and experienced people, who could be used to put the brake on legislation introduced by a Labour Government. But in spite of this the House of Lords is not exactly a popular institution and the Tory Party Head Office, with its eye on the next General Election, would do its best to damp down any action of the House of Lords resulting in any action which might precipitate a political crisis and giving an impetus to a movement to abolish it altogether. So the House of Lords remains discreetly in the background, not anxious to be provocative or do anything that might be an act of suicide. Why should the House of Lords continue to be a part of our Parliamentary institution institutions these days? Is it worth continuing it as a glorified debating society or as a body which can be used by the Government to rectify technical errors in legislation which might have passed unnoticed during its passage through the House of Commons or to make minor changes in Government policy which have been decided on by minor concessions as a result of promises made by Ministers?

Even Sir Alec Douglas-Home, a Conservative if there ever was one, cannot have a great deal of affection and reverence for the House of Lords or he would never have given up his earldom and deserted it. He took the view that the place of the Prime Minister nowadays was in the House of Commons and so divested himself of his ancient titles. So did Lord Hailsham, who had occupied the post of President of the Council and been the Leader of the House of Lords. He was prepared to leave the House of Lords to its fate and to step down to become Mr Quintin Hogg, which at the time he thought might lead to his becoming a Tory Prime Minister.

Then there was the former Earl of Sandwich, who still more formerly was Lord Hinchinbrook. If these distinguished Conservatives had thought that there was any real future for them in the House of Lords they surely would never have left it.

The one went to fight an election in Marylebone and the other to fight one at Accrington, neither of the places being of great historic interest.

If all the other hereditary peers had followed the example of the Earl of Home, Lord Hailsham and the Earl of Sandwich the House of Lords would have liquidated itself and the problem would have been solved. If a Tory Government had been re-elected in 1964 and Sir Alec Douglas-Home had become Prime Minister, and Mr Quintin Hogg been in the Cabinet, and had Mr Montague arrived there too, there might have been quite an exodus of ambitious young earls and viscounts and marquesses and even dukes and princes following their example. The sub-

sequent fate of this trio was not however an encouragement to others. Yet the fact that they were prepared to cast away their coronets and their robes meant that they abolished themselves as lords and they can now have no logical case if a Socialist Government were to argue from this that there was not much point of continuing an institution which distinguished Conservatives regarded with such little respect. No sensible person really takes this hereditary principle seriously these days. The main reason why Mr Heath was elected the Leader of the Tory Party was that the rank and file of the Tory Party wanted to change the image of the party in the eyes of the public and so thought it wise to elbow the old traditional, hereditary, ruling class off the political stage.

Even Mr Harold Macmillan did not take the earldom which was his traditional right as an ex-Prime Minister, objecting like Winston Churchill had done to being buried alive in a political mausoleum and to condemning his son and his grandson to be interred there when their time arrived.

Would it not then be an act of consideration and kindness to young politically-minded peers and heirs to peerages to do the job for them? It would save them from being regarded as traitors to their class or being told that they were just leaving the sinking ship. Better abolish the hereditary peerages altogether and save them the trouble that Sir Alec Douglas Home and Mr Quintin Hogg and Mr Ivor Montague had to take to become commoners?

With Sir Alec Douglas-Home taking the view that the House of Lords had become so irresponsible a body that it was no longer an appropriate place for a Prime Minister to sit in, why should we not now agree that the House of Lords, whose members have no constituencies to report to, should cease to have any power to alter or delay legislation passed by the House of Commons? Has the time not come for a clean amputation, to abolish it altogether or should we let it linger on as a sort of superior debating society which could make polite recommendations and nothing else?

With all the erosions in its powers which took place after its conflicts with the Liberal Government in 1910 and with the Labour Government after the last war it can still waste the time of the House of Commons by moving amendments which it has to consider and could still, on some issue where it thought it was representing public opinion, force a political crisis and make difficulties for a Labour Government if it thought it could get away with it without committing hari-kari.

Recent delaying action by the House of Lords held up the Rent Act and others would have given slum landlords an additional sum of £6,000,000 from the public purse.

Nobody can predict precisely what would happen if some issue moved any large number of the 900 peers to come to the House of Lords to harass or defeat a Labour Government. The problem only arises of course when a Labour Government is in power, for when a Tory Government is in office the House of Lords is somnolent, assuming that no Tory Government is out to threaten the vested interests in land, property and capital which are so strongly entrenched there.

As long as the House of Lords exists a Labour Government must have a certain number of Ministers there to explain its legislation and to carry on its functions, and a certain number of Labour peers as well.

That was the reason why the Labour Party in opposition agreed to some of its members going there as life peers and why Mr Harold Wilson created more life peers who had either been in the House of Commons, or had some knowledge of political and social problems which could be useful in debate. A Labour Prime Minister could in an emergency threaten to create enough peers to vote down diehard Tory mutineers, as Mr Asquith did in his day. That was why the House of Lords in Mr Attlee's day allowed the big measures of nationalisation to go through although it put up a fight on iron and steel. With a Labour Government with a narrower majority the Lords might be tempted to take risks in the hope that in the controversy that followed a General Election might be forced and the Government defeated.

The objection to life peers is in essence the same objection that one has to the others. They are, true, not hereditary, their sons do not succeed them, but they are not elected and are responsible to nobody. The Prime Minister nominates them and it is patronage, giving too much power to a Prime Minister to reward his friends or those he thinks are reliable from his point of view. It might also mean that elderly Members of the House of Commons with their eye on retirement to the Lords might become more amenable and docile towards the Government. Some people prominent in public life accept life peerages because the House of Lords gives them a platform. Take the case of Lord Brockway, who was narrowly defeated by a handful of votes at Eton and Slough. He came to the conclusion that he could still perform some public service and help the cause of the coloured peoples, which he had so long championed, by accepting a life peerage and continuing his propaganda in another part of the building, a task which he has achieved by his earnestness and persistency. One can hardly imagine that ex-colonial secretaries and ex-colonial governors and administrators who had looked upon the House of Lords as their special preserve were enthusiastic when Lord Brockway arrived unexpectedly to continue the debate and his special activities there.

Then there is the case of Lord Soper, who as Dr Donald Soper has been one of the most popular Tower Hill, Trafalgar Square and Hyde Park open-air orators of our generation. The audience in the House of Lords may not be so lively as those that have been accustomed to heckle Lord Soper at the street corners or the dock gates but he at least has a platform and his speeches are more likely to be noticed there by the Press and the radio and can carry his message to a wider audience.

Rev. Dr Soper can claim that he has as much right to be there as the Archbishop of Canterbury and the bishops of the Church of England.

This leads one to the question of the right that the Anglican bishops have to be in the House of Lords at all. Lloyd George in his day of conflict with the Lords used to ask what right the Church of England bishops had to be there any more than the Roman Catholic bishops, or the Free Churches, or the dignitaries of the Church of Scotland, or one might add, the Chief Rabbi or the Salvation Army. There is no real answer to that question for nobody would seriously argue that the Church of England is exclusively representative of the religious life of Britain today. Yet its bishops sit there and sometimes one gets an agreeable surprise when some of them occasionally express comparatively enlightened views.

Do we really need a House of Lords as a revising Chamber to rectify drafting or technical errors in legislation or where the

Government can make last-minute changes in concession to what it admits are valid criticisms?

Some such body may be necessary but it cannot really be argued that the present House of Lords, as it is, is competent to undertake such a task. Only a tenth of its members take an interest in the routine work of the Lords anyway. A committee of the House of Commons in consultation with the clerks of the House and civil servants could do this much better. It would take less time and the whole process of getting legislation on to the Statute Book would be speeded up.

The House of Lords does not often get attacked in the House of Commons these days. It is the convention that 'the other place' must be referred to with respect and deference.

But on May 4th Mr William Hamilton, the outspoken Labour M.P. for West Fife, made a frontal attack when under the Ten Minute Rule he asked 'That leave be given to bring in a Bill to abolish the delaying powers of the House of Lords in respect of legislation'.

One of the main reasons that prompted Mr Hamilton to introduce this Bill was the action of the House of Lords in amending the War Damage Bill in such a way that would have meant that the Burmah Oil Company would have received £4½ million for the damage to its oil installations in Burma during the war with Japan.

Mr Hamilton began his speech by recalling that the Parliament Acts of 1916 and 1949 successfully reduced the power of the House of Lords to delay so that it operated only for one year.

'My view,' he said, 'is that the period is still one year too long. No one could logically defend such a right residing in such an undemocratically unrepresentative, archaic, museum-like Tory-dominated Chamber. My action today is not inspired wholly by the episode of the War Damage Bill on April 13th although I must put it on record that to use a current phrase it "put a tiger in my tank".'

He recalled the fact that the House of Commons had passed the second reading of the Bill by a majority of 93 and that it was also passed in the House of Lords on second reading by 45 votes to 22. 'I ask the House to note those figures,' he continued, '45 to 22. At the Committee Stage of the Bill on 13th April, the

Government were heavily defeated in the House of Lords by a vote of 144 to 69, allegedly on grounds of principle, that retrospective legislation was involved and that the Government were infringing the rule of law.'

Was this the real reason or had the comparative large attendance turned up for the purpose of helping Burmah Oil?

Mr Hamilton had his suspicions and voiced them.

'Having an inquiring nature, I decided to make an analysis of the 144 peers who voted "Consent" on that occasion. I found that 54 of them had not voted that session. Indeed one of them took his seat that very day, and was a Burmah Oil shareholder. The aggregate directorships involved in the case of these 144 amounted to 415, an average of three per peer. These included 110 chairmanships. There were 21 banking directorships; 14 chemicals; 11 property; 7 steel; 6 oil; and the usual Tory "beerage" amounting to 6—a genuine cross section of the British public. One of them, Lord Strathalmond, took his seat in April 1955. He had not opened his mouth there for ten years. Maybe there were good reasons for that. It may be that the reasons were just as good as those for which he attended on April 13th because he was until last December a director of Burmah Oil.'

HON. MEMBERS: Oh.

MR SPEAKER: Order. The hon. Gentleman has full scope to develop his point, but I think that to ensure he is within order he should make clear once and for all now that he is not suggesting that votes were cast in another place because of any unavowed motive. If he makes that clear, he may go on.

MR HAMILTON went on: I was about to come to that point, Mr Speaker. You anticipated me by about three seconds.

I have here a list of the titled shareholders in Burmah Oil. It runs to 60 foolscap pages and about 170 peers are involved. Thirty-eight of them voted, 'Content' on April 13th—a very good word that, 'Content'.

To come to the point you have just raised, Mr Speaker, I am prepared to believe that 38 were motivated solely by a high regard for the rule of law and their dislike of retrospective legislation. I should be very glad to make a supreme effort to believe that their presence in the House of Lords when the Burmah Oil interests were being considered was purely coincidental. It seems to me, on the evidence I have been able to collect, that the House of Lords was not so much acting as a Chamber of Parliament and debating matters of fundamental principle as a shareholders' meeting discussing future

policy. Indeed, I would say that at the last general meeting of the
Burmah Oil Company there were probably fewer shareholders than
there were in the House of Lords——

MR SPEAKER: Order. The point about this is that the other place
is not here to defend itself. I therefore must assume a mantle which
will ensure that no discourtesy as between the Houses should occur.
I would ask the hon. Gentleman to couch his brief explanation of his
Bill—which is all that I am permitted to allow—in terms which
would not be discourteous to the other House of Parliament.

MR HAMILTON: That is an extremely difficult exercise, Mr
Speaker. I am trying to do my best.

The point which I am trying to make is quite simply that, along
the corridor, there is another Chamber which can delay, thwart and
defeat every single bit of legislation which is introduced and passed
by this House. When the Lords claim, as they did on this occasion,
that they were doing it on grounds of high principle, that they
objected to delegated legislation and to the infringement of the rule
of law, that is denied by another case which I shall mention in
passing . . .

I have just given what amounts to the *hors d'oeuvres* about
Burmah Oil. The main meal will come when the Amendments come
back to this House. Meanwhile, I want to put on record what has
happened in the Lords this Session. There have been 10 Divisions
and the Government have been defeated on six occasions. The
average number of defeats per Session during the last 13 years, under
a Tory Government, was two, or, at most, three. In some years it was
never defeated at all. Clearly, they are 'chancing their arm' in this
Session, with the Government constituted as it is.

The intolerable fact, as I have said, is that the House can delay,
thwart and defeat at will any Measure passed and accepted by this
House and in this Parliament. The most controversial legislation is
yet to come—steel, the Lands Commission, and the rest. In my view,
the threat to create a sufficient number of peers to outnumber the
Tories in the other place is no answer. Nor is it sufficient, in my
view, to wait for a mandate, as the Prime Minister himself suggested.
We should accept the challenge now and, if need be, cut the Summer
Recess to do so.

My Bill would be short, simple, unequivocal and moderate. It is in
this conciliatory spirit that I ask leave of the House to introduce it.

Mr Hamilton's Bill was of course stillborn. It had no chance
of getting any further. No Conservative M.P. rose to oppose it
and he was given leave to bring it in.

Its main provisions read:

1.—(1) If a Public Bill, having been passed by the House of

Commons and sent up to the House of Lords at least one month before the end of the session, is rejected by the House of Lords the Bill shall, unless the House of Commons direct to the contrary, be presented to Her Majesty and become an Act of Parliament on the Royal Assent being signified.

(2) A Bill shall be deemed to be rejected by the House of Lords—

    (a) if it is not passed by that House without amendment within one month of its being sent up to the Lords; or

    (b) if having been amended by the Lords within one month of its being sent up to them, the Commons disagree to the amendments made by the Lords.

3. When a Bill is presented to Her Majesty for assent in pursuance of the provisions of this Act, there shall be endorsed on the Bill the certificate of the Speaker of the House of Commons signed by him that the provisions of this Act have been duly complied with.

4. Sections 1 and 2 of the Parliament Act 1911, and the Parliament Act 1949 are hereby repealed.

Mr Hamilton's Bill would have effectively ended the power of the House of Lords to delay legislation.

It was relegated to the parliamentary archives for the time being but it or something like it may soon be needed again.

Mr Hamilton returned to the subject when the House of Commons debated the Lords Amendments to the Burmah Oil Bill and gave a list of the lords who had voted.

There was an unsuccessful attempt by a Conservative M.P., Sir John Foster, to get the Speaker to declare him out of order but the Speaker ruled that he could continue and Mr Hamilton went on.

MR HAMILTON: I am simply putting the facts on the record. If the hon. and learned Member for Northwich (Sir J. Foster) feels that there may be a guilty conscience somewhere, I cannot help that. [HON. MEMBERS: 'Oh.'] All that I am saying is that there is a list, which I have, of peers who are Burmah Oil shareholders and who voted 'Content' in the House of Lords on April 13th. I leave it at that. They are: Lord Amory, Lord Atholl, Lord Baillieu, Lord Boothby, Lord Bridgeman, Lord Chelmer, Lord Cohen, Lord Coleraine, Lord Congleton—all familiar names to some of us—Lord Cornwallis, Lord Craigmyle, Lord Crathorne, Lord Croft, Lord Cullen of Ash-

bourne, Lord Daventry, Lord De La Warr, Lord Digby, Lord
Ebbisham, Lord Falmouth, Lord Godber, Lord Grenfell, Lord Howe,
Lord Ilford, Lord Killearn, Lord Limerick, Lord Meston, Lord Milne,
Lord Morton of Henryton, Lord Reading, Lord Rowallan, Lord
Selkirk, Lord Strathalmond, Lord Strathclyde, Lord Swinton, Lord
Swaythling, Lord Teynham, Lord Verulam, Lord Wrenbury. The
total was 39. Three voted 'Not Content'—Lord Granville-West, Lord
Jessell and Lord Peddie. All credit to them for voting in that lobby.

When right hon. and hon. Members ask me to speak on this
matter about principles of the rule of law and retrospective legislation, I can speak on those subjects. I can speak in legal jargon. But I
speak as an ordinary layman, I hope with some morals and some
principles, and it makes me very angry when, under this kind of
subterfuge, this kind of practice is indulged in. I do not believe that
this argument is being conducted on that high plane. I believe that
it is being used to deceive people into accepting something for other
reasons. The basic reasons——

MR DEPUTY-SPEAKER: Order. The hon. Member was perfectly
entitled to raise the broad issues which he has raised before the
House. But he must not impute improper motive to Members either
in another House or in this House.

MR HAMILTON: The issue is a fairly simple one to my lay mind.
A battle is going on for money out of the public purse by a company
which suffered loss in Burma. Thousands of ordinary humble citizens
also suffered loss. If this House accepts the claim of this company,
because it is wealthy enough to pursue its claim through the courts,
then I shall see to it in any way that I can that every one of my
constituents who suffered in Burma by losing life or limb or bread-
winners will make the same kind of claim on the Government, and I
hope that the Government will accept those claims in the way in
which they are being asked to accept this claim.

That is all that I am asking. This is the political issue which is
involved. Restrictive legislation and the rule of law are, of course,
important and I attach importance to them, but let us not lose sight
of the basic issues.

When the House of Lords had again to consider its attitude to
the amendment there were Tory peers who advised it to persist
and continue its fight for the Burmah Oil shareholders.

Lord Carrington, the Leader of the Conservative Opposition,
advised caution, saying that he doubted 'whether this narrow
issue is of sufficient constitutional importance to merit a head-
on clash between the two Houses'.

Both Lord Fisher, the ex-Archbishop of Canterbury, and the
Marquess of Salisbury also advised caution and urged them to
abstain and not force a fight with the Commons.

Lord Salisbury thought that this was not an issue in which they could fight a great constitutional battle. 'On the contrary,' he said, 'it seems to me that we should be fighting on the worst possible grounds. . . . Indeed I believe that, were we to do so, we might dangerously prejudice the whole position of this House for the future, when the battle for our very existence comes, as I believe it well may, to its full blast.'

This time the diehards were defeated by 74 votes to 26. Discretion was again the better part of valour. The Lords preferred to live to fight another day. After all, compensation for Burmah Oil might not be a popular issue at an election.

But the incident of the House of Lords fight for Burmah Oil, of the advance and retreat, is not without interest.

In writing about the House of Lords in this way it may sound like making an attack on   sick man on his death bed. But if we are going to modernize   rliament we cannot let the House of Lords continue as it   A Labour Government with a tiny majority cannot do   unless the Lords does something so hopelessly reactionary t   commonsense would call for its immediate extinction. A lo   pends on how the Lords behaves towards a Labour Govern   nt hanging on with a slender majority. In any case the Labo   Party should take the precaution of asking the country for   nandate to end it altogether the moment it blocks the way t   necessary and urgent change.

CHAPTER 6

THE BATTLE OF THE FINANCE BILL

In Bernard Shaw's *Major Barbara* there is a conversation between Andrew Undershaft, the armament millionaire, and Lady Britomart about the future of Stephen, his son. He is asked, 'What do you think he had better do?'

Undershaft replies: 'Oh, just what he wants to do. He knows nothing and he thinks he knows everything. That points clearly to a political career. Get him a private secretaryship to someone who can get him an under secretaryship, and then leave him alone. He will find his natural and proper place in the end on the Treasury Bench.'

The young man whose future is being discussed springs up and says, 'I am sorry, sir, that you force me to forget the respect due to you as my father. I am an Englishman and I will not hear the Government of my country insulted.'

Undershaft, with a touch of brutality, replies: 'The government of your country! I am the government of your country! I, and Lazarus. [his partner.] Do you suppose that you and half a dozen amateurs like you, sitting in a row in that foolish gabble ship, can govern Undershaft and Lazarus? No, my friend: you will do what pays us. You will make war when it suits us, and keep peace when it doesn't. You will find out that trade requires certain measures when we have decided on these measures. When I want anything to keep my dividends up, you will discover that my want is a national need. When other people want something to keep my dividends down, you will call out the police and the military. And in return you shall have the support and applause of my newspapers, and the delight of imagining that you are a great statesman. Government of your country! Be off with you, my boy, and play with your caucuses and leading articles and historic parties and great leaders and burning questions and the rest of your toys. I am going back to my country-house to pay the piper and call the tune.'

There have been two world wars since then out of which Undershaft and Lazarus did very well, and since the end of the last war we have spent over £20,000,000,000 on defence, and a dispassionate and objective person could very well argue that Undershaft's analysis of the position, at least as far as the arms industries are concerned, was not so wide of the mark. Only on very rare occasions, as in the Ferranti case, is a Government forced to stand up to a powerful vested interest and demand its money back. Well may we ask the question who governs who?

When a Conservative Government is in power there is no doubt about it. The big, powerful vested interests in finance and industry dictate its policy for they have supplied the money and a Conservative Government is their Government. When the landlords of Britain demanded a Rent Act the Tory Government gave it to them; v ɛn after the defeat of the Labour Government in 1951 the st   asters demanded that the nationalized steel industry shou'   ɔe given back to them the Tory Government obliged; whe   ɪe big aircraft companies wanted big contracts to swell thei   ɔfits and dividends they got them. Whenever during th ast twenty years the Tories have won a General Election   ɛre has been jubilation on the Stock Exchange and shares ¹ ve soared.

If A drew Undershaft had dropped into the House of Commonꞌ ɪny time between 1951 and 1964 he would have made the lacꞌ ɪic comment, 'Same old gabble shop' and gone back to his cꞌ ce realizing that there had been no change. He would have ɔne back to his office quite satisfied that he was still the government.

The General Election of 1964, however, brought a change. The Tory Government had been forced to give way to a Labour Government with a narrow majority and the Tories had crossed the floor to be the Opposition. Nearly all the former Ministers had become company directors. The ex-Prime Minister resumed his role of the Scottish landlord with his 60,000 acres, the ex-Chancellor of the Exchequer, the ex-Minister of Defence, and most of the others were given places on the boards of banks, insurance companies and the big concerns that make substantial profits. Nearly all the Shadow Cabinet were operating on the City Front, some of them with companies doing considerable

business with the Ministries for which they had been responsible and had inside knowledge.

In the House of Commons they clearly showed on every occasion their bitterness and anger because the House of Commons
had become a different place and different people with different
ideas were in their old jobs.

The Labour Government was pledged to introduce a Corporation tax and a Capital Gains tax and to prevent large-scale
evasion of taxation and to reduce businessmen's entertainment
expenses. All this meant revising our system of taxation so that
the largest income section of the nation paid more taxes.

If there had been any doubt about what the Conservative
Party stood for before the Budget was introduced there could
have been none as the Finance Bill made its slow progress on the
floor of the House, taking up the time which could have been
devoted to other legislation. The organization of the parliamentary fight against the Finance Bill was conducted by Mr Edward
Heath, who largely as a result of it, later became Leader of the
Conservative Party when it came to the conclusion that Sir Alec
Douglas-Home had become an election loser and a political
liability. Mr Heath was well qualified for this task because he
had for several years been Government Chief Whip and so had
acquired an intimate knowledge of parliamentary procedure and
so knew all the techniques and tricks that could be used by a
determined Opposition to obstruct and delay.

When it was all over Mr Heath wrote exultantly in an article
in *The Spectator* (23.7.63):

'After 211 hours of debate in twenty-one and a half days the
largest and most complex Finance Bill of modern times has passed
through the House of Commons. In all 1,222 amendments were placed
on the Order Paper, 680 by the Conservative Opposition. There were
108 divisions in three of which the Government was defeated and
one of which it tied (this was the first Government defeat on a
Finance Bill since 1924). Observers agree that it was the most
intensely argued Finance Bill in living memory.

'The time taken by the Bill,' boasted Mr Heath, 'has thrown the
Government business into complete disarray. Although the Whitsun
recess was shortened by eight days and the House will have to sit for
the first week in August and probably longer, the Government has
not been able to find time for three of the major measures mentioned
in the Queen's Speech, Steel Nationalization, the Crown Land

Commission and Leasehold Enfranchisement with two of the political measures, the creation of the Ombudsman and the disclosure of political contributions.'

Nothing could have shown more clearly how the Conservative mind worked or shown the nature of the Conservative Party.

It was out to defend the interests of big business, the Stock Exchange, the big landlords, and the largest income groups, and not only to do this in the Finance Bill but to stave off the legislation objected to by the steelmasters, the property owners and speculators, and also the legislation which would force political parties to disclose the sources of their funds so that the general public would know exactly who paid them.

Mr Heath was entitled to be exultant about the parliamentary fight that had been put up by the Tories on the floor of the House and to expect that the big financial vested interests would pat him on the back and say 'Well done, thou good and faithful servant, enter into the Leadership of the Conservative Party and you will be the next Tory Prime Minister'.

Yet the publicity that the parliamentary fight was receiving in the Press, the radio and the TV also resulted in the public asking the question what the fight was about, and it was impossible to hide the fact that the fight was for a very small fraction, the wealthiest fraction of the population, the rest.

The more sensational Press found the technicalities of the debate on the Finance Bill too dull for its readers, who knew that a big fight was going on but not exactly what it was all about.

It was the *Guardian*, in a leading article 'Why Tighten the Tax Net?', that put the issues clearly on June 3rd when the vote was equal and when, according to tradition, the chairman gave his casting vote to the Government.

'The row about the Corporation tax is deafening—and last night's tied vote will add to it again—but it has little to do with ordinary political argument. Its cause is a simple matter of commerce. The Government is proposing to change a situation in which the largest company in Britain (Shell), the third largest (BP), and a number of others have paid virtually no British income tax since 1960. It is a state of affairs which the Government wants to change in the interests of fairness. The companies naturally would like to preserve it, for no one enjoys giving up a privilege. There was bound to be a row. Mr Callaghan and the oil companies between them have merely proved once more that Burke was right: "To tax and to please ... is not given to men."'

The article went on to say that other companies were affected but that the oil companies were protesting the loudest.

'Shell and BP, however, are the largest and can be expected to make the loudest noise because their case is an extreme one. For four of the past five years the "net UK rate" at which Shell has been paying income tax in Britain has been one penny in the pound; in the fifth year it paid no tax at all. BP paid no tax at all throughout the five-year period. Both companies own and operate immense quantities of plant and equipment in Britain and enjoy the benefits of all the available public services, as well as making "great claims on the Government" (as the Financial Secretary to the Treasury put it) for the defence of their installations. Both companies, however, have been able to avoid paying British taxes because Britain, unlike any other major industrial country, forgives shareholders their domestic taxes if their company has already paid taxes abroad.

'Making the oil companies pay their taxes is, however, only one of the purposes of the Corporation tax. Another of the Government's aims, with this tax as with others, is to make it more profitable for companies to invest at home as well as abroad. It is not merely the foreign exchange consideration—investment by Shell added to last year's balance of payments' deficit—but also the fact that many branches of British industry and, above all, many parts of Britain itself need more capital than they have been getting. There must be more productive investment at home if Britain is to be modernized and to become prosperous. The truth of this may be more obvious to people who live north of the Trent than to Londoners, but it is true all the same and the Government must not overlook it. Fifty per cent of the population, after all, live in the North, and only four per cent of the whole own shares.

'To the non-capitalists, ninety-six per cent, Corporation tax is personally irrelevant. Their need is for housing, education, and employment—and a reasonably stable cost of living. These must be a first care of any Government that claims to govern properly and that wants to survive. The Corporation tax is one of the Government's means towards meeting those needs.'

The main debate was soon confined to the specialists on both sides. The Government, anxious to get the Bill through, discouraged speeches from its own side and the Tories had more experts on the intricacies of company finance.

In the House of Commons there is a tradition (but not a rule) that Members should disclose their financial interests when they speak in a debate where they may be affected. That was only rarely done in the debate on the Finance Bill. When the question was raised on a point of order the chairman explained that it was a custom but he had no power to call upon a Member to declare whether he was a director or a shareholder in any company that would have to pay increased taxation or how much he stood to gain if the amendment he was supporting were to be carried.

After that the custom was ignored.

Nobody said 'I am a shareholder and a director of companies which have a lot to gain if this amendment is carried and I estimate that if it is, I shall be better off by about £1,000 a year'.

The Standing Orders of the House of Commons should be altered to make it obligatory on a Member to do this. Had it been so during the Finance Bill Hansard next day would have read very much like the *Directory of Directors*.

Members of the House of Commons are supposed to speak for their constituents but all the arguments were, as the *Guardian* pointed out, for the six per cent of the population that owned shares in the companies involved. Never were so many speeches made for the benefit of so few.

The Chancellor of the Exchequer could have been excused if looking across at the other side of the House he imagined he was still meeting deputations from the Institute of Directors or the Federation of British Industries.

When he did so in a speech reported in the *Daily Telegraph* (5.7.65), Sir Robert Cary, M.P. for Withington, Manchester, raised the matter in the House as a breach of privilege.

Mr Callaghan had said:

'He did not think of them as the honourable Member for X or Y or Z. I look at them and say Investment Trusts, capital speculators or "That is the fellow who is the Stock Exchange man who makes profit on Gilt Edged". I have almost forgotten their constituencies, but I shall never forget their interests. I wonder sometimes whom they represent? Their constituencies or their friends' particular interests.'

The Speaker ruled next day that this was a *prima facie* case that should go to the Committee of Privileges and when the

Leader of the House moved this there was a lively debate after which the motion was only carried by a majority of six.

If Andrew Undershaft had been in the gallery he would have wondered what all the fuss was about.

Of course the Committee of Privileges did nothing about Mr Callaghan. A large number of Labour M.P.s went to their constituencies the next weekend and repeated the offending paragraph from the Chancellor's speech and the matter was discretely dropped. But this issue had pinpointed the real issue of the Finance Bill more than all the speeches that had gone on all day and all night.

It was the Conservative *Sunday Telegraph* (13.6.65) that best summed up the character of the Opposition to the Finance Bill in an article headed 'Tories Mobilise their Stockbroker Storm Troops'. It said:

'If it wasn't for the constant possibility of a tie, or even a Government defeat, the debates in committee on the Finance Bill, which dominated Parliament for three weeks before the Whitsun recess and continue the day after tomorrow, would have bored all but the most fervent financial experts. Hansard, usually the most entertaining of daily publications, cramps the intellect with financial jargon. . . .

'The majority of Conservatives who have taken part in the debate hold down a company directorship or have some declared interest in property or land. The two most vocal opponents of the Bill have been Sir Douglas Glover (Ormskirk), a director of a finance company, with a long record of executive posts in Lancashire drapery, and Mr Peter Walker (Worcester), a young insurance broker and director of 11 companies.

'These two, with 18 speeches each, are far ahead of the rest of the field, but they have been ably supported, for instance, by Mr John Hall (Wycombe), 12 speeches, 11 directorships; Mr Geoffrey Hirst (Shipley), 9 speeches, 5 directorships; Sir Arthur Vere Harvey (Macclesfield), 7 speeches, 12 directorships; and Sir Henry d'Avigdor Goldsmid (Walsall South), 5 speeches, 6 directorships.

'Nor have the Conservatives lacked firm experience in the Stock Exchange and its subsidiaries. Sir Alexander Spearman (Scarborough and Whitby), a partner in a firm of London stockbrokers, has been a virulent opponent of the Finance Bill, as have Mr Nigel Birch (Flint West), an ex-London stockbroker, Mr Peter Hordern (Horsham), a London stockbroker, Mr John Tilney (Liverpool, Wavertree), a stockbroker from Liverpool, Mr David Webster (Weston-super-Mare), a stockbroker from Somerset, and Mr Donald Box (Cardiff North), a stockbroker from Cardiff.'

When the Finance Bill was finally passed I placed the following motion on the House of Commons Order Paper:

'That this House, recalling the historic words of Sir Winston Churchill that "The Conservative Party is not a party but a conspiracy", his assertion that it stood for "the great vested interests banded together in a formidable federation; corruption at home, aggression to cover it up abroad, the trickery of tariff juggles, the tyranny of a party machine, sentiment by the bucketful, patriotism by the imperial pint, the open hand at the public exchequer, the open door at the public house, dear food for the million, cheap labour for the millionaire" and his warning that "the Conservative Party is nothing less than a deliberate attempt on the part of important sections of the propertied classes to transfer their burdens to the shoulders of the masses of the people and to gain greater profits for the investment of their capital by charging higher prices", notes that in the debates on the Finance Bill the Conservative Party has continued its traditional role.'

CHAPTER 7

M.P.S AS PAVLOV'S DOGS

The very fact that the Government had such a tiny majority, which illness or accident might end any night and precipitate a General Election, made people not normally interested in politics pay greater attention to what was going on at Westminster than they had done for a decade.

This was reflected in the articles that began to appear in the Press. During the thirteen years of Conservative Government there had not been much discussion of the procedure of the House of Commons. The Government had a comfortable majority and there was no prospect of a General Election unless the Prime Minister and the Government wanted it.

But the result of the General Election of 1964 had changed this. In the early part of 1965 the public opinion polls began to go against the Labour Government and the large-scale betting against the chances of the Government surviving indicated how uncertain the political situation had become.

If M.P.s went into hospital even for a check-up or for some minor ailment the fact became front page news along with the figures of his majority at the last election.

People began to wonder why it was necessary for the House of Commons to spend day after day discussing the never-ending Finance Bill.

The commentators began to ask why the Finance Bill could not be considered in Committee so that the House could go on with other business.

Some of us had been asking this question for years and were surprised when we began to get unexpected support. On June 25th the political correspondent of *The Times* wrote:

'Much of current Labour criticism of parliamentary procedure and practice runs the risk of losing sympathy for the sounder proposals for reform. As it happens, the Financial Bill now passing through the Commons shows where the main fault lies in the system and suggests how easily it could be righted.

'When he was Leader of the House Mr Iain Macleod came to the conclusion that there was only one way to give the Commons more elbow room for both legislation and important debates. That was to shift the Committee stage of the Finance Bill from the floor of the House and send it to a Standing Committee upstairs, like many other Bills.

'The argument is as substantial today as it was then. Apart from the four days of the debate on the Chancellor's Budget statement, the Finance Bill has had one day for second reading and twelve days in Committee. Three more Committee days are set down for this week and the Government cannot yet be sure that this will be enough to complete the Committee stage. Then there will be two days (as the Government suggest) or three or four days (as the Opposition hope) for report stage and one day for third reading.

'Leave aside the Budget debate and the Finance Bill will have taken the Commons 20 days. This is about one-sixth of the whole of Government time in a session of normal length—that is, of between 160 to 170 days. It is true that Mr Callaghan's first Budget is the longest in parliamentary memory and complicated into the bargain. But almost any Finance Bill will take about 15 parliamentary days, one way or another.

'The classic argument for keeping the Bill on the floor is, of course, that nothing the Commons do is more important than this, and that every Member should have his right to a voice and a vote on it. But what has happened this year in practice? Apart from a few periods when three-line whips were applied, Government and Opposition have worked rotas that kept only about half the M.P.s in full attendance. . . .

'In this way, disregarding the marching and counter-marching of the divisions, the Finance Bill has in effect been taken this year in a Standing Committee, with complete efficiency and representativeness. But if it had been sent upstairs to a Standing Committee, the House would have had 20 days to spare, not only for legislation but for general debates in which the Commons could have given a lead on domestic issues and foreign affairs, and perhaps have begun to rival "Panorama" in conference.'

As the political correspondent of *The Times* pointed out, the rota system by which both parties agreed to organize attendance and votes by shifts, with some Members being allowed to pair on certain nights of the week, the idea that it was constitutionally important for every Member to be present had been thrown overboard. It was only a formality to say that the whole House was sitting and all the M.P.s were listening to the arguments, often so technical that only a chartered accountant could completely understand them.

The numbers that remained on either side could easily have been accommodated in one of the committee rooms. The party whips were there to see that when voting time came, the M.P.s who were on duty rolled up. Afterwards they went back to the library, or the smoke room, or the tea room, or wherever they could find a spot to rest or sleep. It would be gross exaggeration to say that ten per cent of the Members heard all the arguments during the days and nights that the House nominally devoted to the consideration of the Finance Bill.

A Conservative M.P., Mr W. F. Deedes, the Member for Ashford, gave his impressions of one of these all-night sessions in the *Sunday Telegraph* (27.6.25). What do M.P.s do when they are not in the Chamber during the night, he asked.

'And where else, it may be asked, might Members be? All Ministers have rooms and so the option of a settee. These objects, on which it is possible to sleep only on your back, give rise to some of the worst nightmares I have experienced.

'An increasing number of M.P.s have rooms of their own and can rest there. I do not recommend lonely catnaps, broken by bells, in these cells. Nothing lowers morale faster.

'For the rest, there are a dozen deep armchairs in the library, which for some curious reason attract all those who snore loudest; seating for 50 in the smoke room; for another 30 or so in the tea room. The rest of the place is furnished exactly like a railway station waiting-room.

'To nap or not to nap? It is a hard question. To eat or not to eat? That is even harder. From midnight onwards the canteen will offer eggs and bacon. The tea room does a roaring trade in a particular brand of night drink. Tea and coffee too, of course. . . .

'Deepest depression comes to me not in the small hours before dawn, but at 1 a.m. This is a common experience. A canvass on the prospects then invariably draws dismal forebodings. Even the police and badge messengers, apostles of the disciplined approach to all-night sittings, look forlorn.

'It is, of course, the hour when those of normal habits should be dropping into deepest sleep and are most missing it. If dinner has not been digested, it makes this known about 1 a.m.

'By 3 a.m. one feels better. Fading hope has given way to certainty and resolve. Soon after, in high summer, the new Member sees his first dawn from the terrace, the equivalent of being blooded while fox-hunting.'

I had not thought of the analogy with fox hunting myself but I understood what this bored and exhausted Tory M.P. meant.

From another angle a new Labour M.P., Mrs Shirley Williams, M.P. for Hitchin, wrote in the *Observer* (8.8.65).

'At long last, what must be the most exhausting session of any Parliament in modern times has ground to a close. For three months M.P.s can join the world of normal people, sleep soundly in bed at night, and can read about the illnesses or the thundering consciences of their colleagues as news and not as bulletins for the front line.

'There have been sudden alarums, moments of melodrama, rumours running through the House like wind in wheat. But the dominant mood has been that of the wartime shelters. There is a kind of stoical satisfaction in sitting up all night, drinking tea and aimlessly gossiping, and letting it be known that one has been through the night watch. And then one is suddenly aware that this is a crazy ritual sacrifice. I remember one night in which an elderly M.P. drifted quietly from room to room, unable to sit down because of spinal trouble; a few days later he was among the Parliamentary invalids.

'There is a kind of barrack-room comradeship. The job of the Government whips is nerve-racking, but they have been able to work more by cajolery and by appeals to loyalty than by wielding the big stick. The Parliamentary Labour Party is an odd animal, and reacts in all sorts of unexpected ways to threats; on the whole, the whips have been wise.

'In the long nights in the great neo-gothic palace most of us realize how cut off we are from the city outside. We lose touch. The peculiar parliamentary game with its unwritten customs and its tyrannical traditions is part of a private world. The new M.P.s in particular resent this. So the reform of parliamentary procedure has become a central issue for them.'

As one who had been in Parliament for nearly twenty years it was very encouraging to see a young M.P. writing like this and still more to read that other older M.P.s shared these opinions:

'Some of the older parliamentary hands feel that the constitutional baby may be thrown out with the bathwater; but there is plenty of support high up, too. One senior Minister — usually described as a Gaitskellite — denounced a group of his young supporters one night: "Why the devil don't you get on with the real job of reform? Why do I have to look to the Left for it?" He was thinking of the new M.P.s who have made reform of procedure their special interest—David Kerr, Trevor Park, David Ensor and others. "I hope to heaven you youngsters put a bomb under this place," a junior Minister said to me last week. After watching the sad little procession of sick Members, the stretchers and the beds made up in

Ministers' rooms for those unable even to walk, one feels that the private game has gone on too long and has been ludicrously savage.'

Now when junior Ministers encourage new M.P.s 'to put a bomb under this place' we appear to be getting on. But how far are these complaints from the old fox-hunting Tory M.P. and the enthusiastic young Labour M.P. likely to get us?

As for the Tory M.P.s, there has never been any real sign that they want to change the procedure of the House of Commons. The present procedure suits them. They do not want to come to the House at 10.30 in the morning. Many of them are directors of companies, business men, engaged in buying and selling property, on the Stock Exchange or in their lawyers' offices. From their point of view the less work the House of Commons does, the fewer times it meets, the longer its recesses and vacations, the better it suits them. They do not want a House of Commons poking into their affairs, or restricting their activities, or passing legislation which reduces their profits, or interferes with big business or high finance. Of course they do not want to dispense with Parliament altogether. It preserves the pretence that we are a democracy and not a plutocratic dictatorship. As long as a government takes its instructions from the City, the banks, big business, the Property Owners' Association and the Federation of British Industries, what need is there for them to bother about modernizing Parliament?

One cannot expect a Labour Government with a tiny majority to go in for drastic parliamentary reform either. It needs all its time for pushing its programme through with measures which will get it back into power at the next General Election.

All this is defensible and understandable. The public outside doesn't understand the technicalities of parliamentary procedure anyway. So it will require a Labour Government with a substantial working majority to overhaul the House of Commons.

But the way has to be prepared for it, otherwise the old frustrations and futilities will go on and bring Parliament into contempt.

Fortunately there are voices raised outside with warnings from those who, while not in the House of Commons, are keeping a watchful eye on it.

Commenting on the proceedings of the Committee stage of the Finance Bill, the *Economist* (12.6.65) said:

'The whole process has been an outstanding example of the inefficiency of the British parliamentary system. Apart from the two front benches and a few specialists on both sides, the Chamber has for much of the time contained very few Members. Somewhere in the building, however, around 300 more had to be kept ready at all hours to perform the ritual of voting. It is doubtful if more than a couple of dozen of them played any part in the debate.

It urged that in future years the Finance Bill should be taken in a Committee upstairs.

'A special committee would have to be set up consisting of the Treasury and Board of Trade Ministers and their Opposition counterparts. One system worth keeping in mind is that of the United States Congress, where the House Ways and Means Committee (containing 25 congressmen out of 435) and the Senate Finance Committee (18 senators out of 100) go through the details of tax bills before they pass on to the floor of the House or the Senate, where they can sometimes be approved without too much discussion. A Commons finance committee should probably consist therefore of between 40 and 60 (out of 630) Members. It should also be given the right, which the American committees possess and freely use, to summon any expert witnesses from outside the House. This would be a considerable improvement on the present method by which Members of Parliament unofficially represent interests whose case they often imperfectly understand. But the main fault of the American committees, that they are inclined to take an interminable time framing and amending tax bills, would be avoided. For the committee on the Finance Bill could not deliberate too long, since the Bill has to be on the statute book before the beginning of August if taxes are to be levied.'

Yet one cannot see such a commonsense proposal getting through the House of Commons without a struggle. Although it was crystal clear after the experience of the Finance Bill of 1965 that taking the Finance Bill on the floor of the House meant an enormous waste of time and energy, it is a break with tradition and tradition in the House of Commons dies hard.

Mr Rudolf Klein, the Home Editor of the *Observer* (23.5.65), made very much the same points.

To ask M.P.s to vote on a measure like the Finance Bill, he

argued, is rather like asking them to vote on the merits of the quantum theory.

'Yet such is the peculiarity of our parliamentary system that this is precisely what the average M.P. is required to do—or, rather, to pretend to do. As a result, he is reduced to the level of Pavlov's dog: he reacts simply to the sound of the division bell summoning him to vote. He may have no special interest in the subject at issue. All that concerns him is that his party should vote its full strength.'

Many people have been arraigned before the Committee of Privileges for less than that. If to be compared with Pavlov's dogs is not a breach of privilege what is?

But it was so true that nobody challenged it and nobody knows how true it is better than the Members of the House of Commons. They have said it themselves over and over again.

The critic in the *Observer* went on to apply the lesson of the Finance Bill to other legislation and argued the case for allowing M.P.s to investigate subjects *before* the Government is committed to every detail of a new Bill. So many policy decisions nowadays demand knowledge of a specialized character. He concluded:

'But, just because M.P.s generally lack such specialized knowledge or the means of acquiring it, there is growing cynicism about their role. Too many Commons debates seem plain irrelevant.

'This, perhaps, is the strongest single argument for giving M.P.s the opportunity to inform themselves: so as to fortify Parliament's prestige and prevent the waste of time and effort typified by the Finance Bill. But there would be incidental benefits, too.

'Ministers might no longer have to spend long nights in the House and emerge exhausted to tackle their daily duties. And M.P.s, actually given something to do and feeling themselves to be more than lobby-fodder, might indulge less in the petty back-biting which so often is now their only escape from the frustrations of life on the back benches.'

Many M.P.s must have thought that the article summed up what many of them felt.

He had, however, made one slip. He had begun his article by saying, 'For much of last week, while the eloquence of a handful of M.P.s spent itself on a waste of empty *red* leather benches, a stage army of bleary eyed M.P.s trooped in and out of the division lobbies through the early hours of the morning : voting on a debate which the great majority had not even heard'.

The description was accurate except for one point. The benches in the House of Commons are green. It is the House of Lords benches that are red.

It enabled the Leader of the House and the Lord President of the Council to say, triumphantly, later on :

'The degree of knowledge outside the House about our procedures is abysmally low. I read an article in a newspaper by a man who criticized our procedures and criticized honourable Members sitting here on our red benches. He had obviously not even seen the Chamber.'

Did it really matter to the argument whether the colour of the benches was green, red or red, white and blue? Asked for his comment on this Mr Klein replied :

My reply to his peculiarly ill-natured smear is :
(1) I frequently attend House of Commons debates. My mistake about the colour of the benches was one of those unfortunate lapses from which, I presume, even Mr Bowden is not immune.
(2) I have studied the whole subject of parliamentary reform for some time (cf. my appendix in Bernard Crick's book) and discussed it with a large number of academics, M.P.s and others concerned.
(3) My own opinion of Mr Bowden's obscurantist attitude towards parliamentary reform is mild compared with that expressed in private by some of his Cabinet colleagues with whom I have discussed it.

CHAPTER 8

AMATEURS AND PROFESSIONALS

Should the House of Commons try to avoid the necessity of all-night sittings by meeting at an earlier hour than the 2.30 that has been its custom for so many years?

This question was debated at some length when the Abolition of Murder Bill was being discussed by Parliament.

After the Bill had been passed by a considerable majority on Second Reading it was then decided, after a vote, to send it upstairs for the Committee stage.

I was a member of this Committee and heard the old familiar arguments gone over again. We spent four mornings from 10.30 to one o'clock discussing the Opposition's amendments and then, late on a Friday afternoon when most Members had gone home as usual, a private Member's motion to bring it back to the floor of the House was carried by a small majority. This presented a problem to the Government already pressed for time for its other business and did not wish to have it take up valuable days which had already been set aside for other legislation.

To have the Finance Bill and the Abolition of Murder Bill, which offered so much opportunity for lengthy time-wasting and distractive speeches, would have meant almost a complete bottleneck.

The Government could have again asked the House to send it back to the Committee which had spent four mornings on it already and resume its deliberations at the point where they had been interrupted. That, some of us thought, would have been the wisest and firmest action. But the Government took the view that it would accept the decision to bring back the discussion to the floor of the House but that instead of this taking place in the afternoons it should take place on Wednesday mornings.

There was a debate on this in which the Conservative Opposition stated their case against the House meeting to discuss this business in the morning.

The former Tory Chief Whip, Sir Martin Redmayne, spoke for over half an hour objecting to the idea of asking the House to sit on Wednesday mornings.

He said that 'at the very best the promoters of the Bill could not hope to see the Bill through the Committee stage in less than nine or twelve weeks.

He added, 'I say quite seriously that these morning sittings will not be Parliament in the sense of Parliament assembled because the difficulties which will free Members in attending will be too great', and went on to argue from his very wide experience as Government Chief Whip that it was a hardship for everybody from Ministers to the clerks of the House and the 'ladies who clean up the mess we leave every day' to ask the House to meet on Wednesday mornings. 'The Press', he said, 'would have to work extra shifts to report us. All these people will have to be here. So too will the staff of the Official Report, the engineers, the boiler room men and others.' It did not occur to him that some of these would welcome overtime or that it might mean some additional employment.

It certainly took a little credulity to be convinced that the Chief ex-Whip was mainly concerned about the boilermen and the engineers and the tea room staff. One wondered how often he had consulted them during his term of office. But one certainly could understand his difficulties with Tory M.P.s for a great deal of his work had been getting them to turn up at the House of Commons not only on Wednesday mornings but Wednesday and Thursday nights as well.

When I was outside the Parliamentary Labour Party I sometimes acted as an unofficial teller at divisions at ten o'clock and watched the Tory M.P.s come through the lobby. It was always a revelation to me. There were the M.P.s that I did not recognize, those I had never seen before and others whom I had assumed were dead or had lost their seats at the last Election or had gone to the House of Lords.

During the years of the Macmillan Government when the Tories had a sizeable majority there were large numbers who only turned up at ten o'clock to vote on the occasion of three-line whips, who never made speeches or asked questions or even took the trouble to listen to the debates. Of course the ex-Chief Whip knew this and so the thought of having to get these very occasional attenders at Westminster to attend on Wednesday mornings seemed an insoluble problem. As a matter of fact it turned out that the attendance on the Wednesday mornings to vote on the issues contained in the Murder—Abolition of Death Penalty Bill, about which we were told the public outside were deeply distressed, was very meagre indeed.

He was followed by Mr Fred Blackburn (the Member for Stalybridge and Hyde), who had long experience of morning sessions of the House as one of the chairmen of Standing Committees. He expressed the view that the floor of the House was not the place to discuss the details of a Bill.

'I do not think,' he said, 'that 630 people wandering in and out are a competent body to discuss the details of the Committee stage of a Bill. Therefore my view, which I think is generally known in the House, is that the Committee stage of every Bill—including the Finance Bill—should be sent to a Standing Committee in order to give more time on the floor of the House for any of the debates which at present we are not able to have.'

The debate was interesting because it revealed the Tory antipathy to change in the ancient routine of the House. But it was not so ancient. It was not a law of nature that the House of Commons must meet at 2.30 in the afternoon. A little research revealed that in the years gone by the House had met at very early hours indeed. During the time of the 1745 Rebellion it had met at six o'clock in the morning, when it passed the Regicide Bill it met at eight, which appears to have been quite a usual time for that period. The ex-Attorney General drew my attention to the fact that when Strafford was tried for high treason in Westminster Hall the proceedings began at eight.

In those days of course there were difficulties about artificial light and there was much less business. But during the last war the House began its sittings in the mornings and now it meets in the morning on Fridays.

All the arguments reverted to the one that many M.P.s were too occupied in the mornings with other private business, the lawyers were busy at their chambers or in the courts and those with financial interests were occupied in the City or in the boardrooms, or at the Stock Exchange. They had to make their money there, the nation's business could come afterwards.

It was left for Mr Herbert Bowden, the Leader of the House, to put the position quite clearly.

'The point was made by the right hon. Gentleman the Member for Thirsk and Malton and others about the inconvenience to the House of sitting in the mornings. I accept that it is an inconvenience to sit in the mornings. It is an inconvenience to those who have something else to do, and it may not be as convenient for Ministers who have appointments, and so on. It may not be as convenient to Members who have to be in court in the mornings. It may not be as convenient to doctors who are in their surgeries in the mornings. But, surely, in all these things Parliament must come first. If we really argue that the hours of the Sittings of Parliament must be adjusted to suit the convenience of all Members at all times, we should be sitting some peculiar hours. Parliament must come first, and Members must adjust their lives and their interests outside to suit the hours of Parliament.

'I was asked why, in the view of the Government, it was thought necessary to have free votes on the Bill, and why we are not to adopt it as a Government Bill. The answer is simple. The answer is that on this side of the House we are of the opinion that there are many measures — I am thinking particularly of Sunday observance, measures of that sort—which are not party political measures at all. There is a great deal which ought to be done. The Government could introduce a Bill; a private Member could introduce a Bill; the decision on the issue must be by a free vote of the House. That is our view, and that is what we shall do on a number of occasions as legislation comes along.'

From the national point of view what is wrong with that?

How many M.P.s tell their constituents at an election time or state in their election addresses that they are going to Parliament to place their own private interests before those of the people they are asking to return them to Parliament?

How many of them say, 'I must warn you ladies and gentlemen that I cannot possibly give you full-time service. My main preoccupation must be to earn money somewhere else. It is ridiculous to ask me to work in the House of Commons in the mornings. You must be content to have my services half-time or quarter-time or even less than that.'

The position was put quite clearly in an article entitled 'What Sort of Parliament' by Arthur Blenkinsop, M.P., in The Spectator (19.1.65):

'The main objection to morning sittings is not the interference that this would cause to Ministers, nor to the other business of Parliament, but rather its interference with Members' other interests outside Parliament. The 1959 report of the Select Committee phrased the matter very delicately: "The Committee agree unanimously that the claims of the House must be always paramount and that therefore the business of the House and the duties which membership imposes upon all who are elected to Parliament must always take precedence over all other demands upon a Member's time. Nevertheless, there are bound to be differing views as to whether membership of the House of Commons would be served better by retaining Members within her ranks who bring to her deliberations the benefit of their knowledge and experience derived from other fields during such hours of the day as their attendance can be spared from the precincts of Westminster." What a lot of humbug! So parliamentary duties are supposed to take precedence, but not, of course, over other business and professional interests that involve regular absence from Parliament in the mornings! In fact, the procedures of Parliament have been forced into the strait-jacket of the present unnatural timetable to suit the convenience of Members who have never recognized the precedence of their Parliamentary duties. Members in the past have been unwilling to serve on Standing Committees that meet in the mornings, and membership of these committees has for years been largely restricted to those who are stigmatized as full-time, or professional, Members. I believe that in recent years no more than seventy Members have attended morning committee meetings at all frequently and not more than about 200 have attended at all. Indeed, it was in part to meet this difficulty that the size of these committees was reduced. The financial difficulties that forced many Members to find additional income from other part-time work have now been overcome. It should therefore now be possible to look at the matter afresh.'

I think in this matter Mr Blenkinsop expressed the view of most Labour M.P.s. There are of course lawyers and company directors, business men and doctors among Labour M.P.s, but only a small fraction of them.

Most of them belong to occupations which are impossible for them to carry on when they enter Parliament. That was one of the arguments used by the Lawrence Committee in recommending an increase in M.P's pay. It is impossible for a miner, an engineer, a teacher, an engine driver, a building worker to continue his old job when he comes to the House of Commons.

Has the House of Commons not become, with the enormous variety of problems an M.P. has to deal with, a full-time job and are not his constituents entitled to ask him to place his duties to his constituents first?

Of course it is impossible to lay down the hard and fast rule that an M.P. should be an M.P. and nothing else. If a constituency decided to return an M.P. who tells them quite frankly what his other interests are and how they are likely to conflict with his duties to them when he becomes a Member of Parliament, then the constituencies can have no complaint if they find that their M.P. spends most of his time away from Parliament, never agrees to serve on a committee but merely turns up occasionally on a three-line whip.

How many M.P.s told the electors at the last Election or will tell them at the next: 'I am your M.P. but my main purpose in Parliament will be to defend the interests of my company, the bank, the insurance company, the financial house, the aircraft companies, the brewers, distillers, investment concerns and property concerns with which I and my colleagues are connected'? Or are these matters discreetly kept in the background until the Election is over?

On the other hand, when they come up for re-election as directors do they tell the shareholders, 'I am sorry but I cannot look after your business as much as I would like to because I am a busy M.P. and have to be absent in the House of Commons a lot of my time looking after the interests of my constituents and not of the shareholders. Please accept my apologies for having been absent from so many directors' meetings and the annual general meeting because they were held on the same day as important debates in the House or when deputations of my constituents came to lobby me'?

Or he may argue 'I was looking after your interests on the day the House was discussing the Corporation Tax and the Capital Gains Tax and business expenses. And I did it so well that even the Chancellor of the Exchequer thought of me not as the Member for ———— but the spokesman for Big Business and the Stock Exchange. I deserve every penny of my director's fees. Indeed I deserve a rise.'

The M.P. may argue at a political meeting that he is serving his constituents or at a meeting of his shareholders that he is representing them, but it is rather difficult for him to explain how he can do both at the same time.

Let us take the example of a well-known M.P. who is both busily engaged in politics and business. In the Tory Government

Mr Reginald Maudling was Chancellor of the Exchequer and when he left the Treasury he became a director of the Associated Electrical Industries and the Dunlop Rubber Company.

To be an efficient director of one of these companies one would have thought would be an exacting, full-time job. But Mr Maudling also became a leading member of Mr Heath's Shadow Cabinet, being allocated Foreign Affairs. One would have thought that would have been very much a full-time job too, but obviously Mr Maudling is a glutton for work.

Indeed one might ask, 'Is not membership of the Shadow Cabinet very much of a full-time job too'. Is it really possible for even a super politician like Mr Maudling to follow what is happening in America, or in China, Russia, Japan and Europe while concentrating on the affairs of the Associated Electric Company and Dunlops?

Most of the Shadow Cabinet are in the same position with what must be conflicting loyalties in time and energy to business and to the House of Commons. How can it possibly be done?

Now, in Britain, Cabinet Ministers give up their directorships and business interests when they take office. A good case could be made for Shadow Cabinet Ministers being made to do this too. But at this there will be a cry, 'Oh stop. This serving the country business, this political patriotism is going too far. What are we to live on?' The answer is that £3,500 a year has been fixed as a sufficient salary for a full-time M.P. Small as this sum may seem to a company director, it is a great deal more than what is paid to ninety-five per cent of the constituents whom M.P.s are supposed to represent in Parliament.

As Mr Blenkinsop said in the conclusion of his article:

'But it is argued that the contacts from regular outside work invigorate Parliament and prevent Members becoming isolated. What hypocritical nonsense this is, at least when it is advanced in defence of Members earning their major income from work outside Parliament! Of course regular outside contacts are valuable, indeed, vital, for members if they are to be effective. But this does not necessitate other paid employment. Very many of our so-called full-time, professional politicians give voluntary service to a host of organizations, both statutory and voluntary. Surely membership of hospital management committees, for example, can be as valuable to the House as highly paid posts on the boards of one or other of the finance houses or industrial concerns that today seem to provide an automatic home for defeated Ministers. I am not arguing that outside interests, whether paid or not, should be prohibited. Simply that the present position should be recognized for what it is and that those who in fact give only part of their time to Parliament should not claim any special virtue.

'I feel it is ridiculous, when we are all anxious that we should look afresh at our old-established customs and practices in industry, that we should tolerate arrangements in Parliament that tend to bring the whole institution into some public contempt when the reforms are in our own hands.'

What is the Tory reply to this? Alongside Mr Blenkinsop's article there appeared another by Mr Edward Gardner, the Conservative M.P. for Billericay. It was entitled 'A Peril Best Avoided', the peril being that Parliament might become a full-time job. Mr Gardner asked:

'The increase in parliamentary salaries has revived the argument that membership of the House of Commons should be a full-time professional occupation. This raises a problem that has been the uneasy concern of politicians of all parties at Westminster for nearly half a century. What kind of a Member of Parliament does the country want? Does it want a House of Commons filled with professional politicians dependent for their living and way of life upon the constant approval or the whim of their party, or does it want Members of the widest experience with the best-known guarantee for an active conscience—financial independence?'

Mr Gardner feels strongly that M.P.s should not be professional politicians. He obviously thinks that he should be classified as one of the amateurs and regards the professionals at Westminster as the Gentlemen at Lords regard the Players. He represents Billericay, an Essex county constituency with over 52,000 electors, and is in with a minority vote. One would think that looking after Billericay under these conditions would be in the way of a full-time job. But he disagrees with the Socialists who contend that it should be one. 'Indeed,' he says, 'the very word professional is something of a discord in the spirit, tradition and history of the House of Commons.' Substitute the word 'cricket' for the House of Commons and you have the traditional Lords snob, accustomed to looking down their noses at the Players even when they score more runs and field better than they do. The House of Commons, however, is run by professionals. The Speaker is a full-time professional. He has to be there in order to do the job. So is the Chairman of Committees, the Deputy Speaker, who if he is a lawyer, cannot act as a professional against a Member. The Sergeant-at-Arms is a professional and so is the Speaker's Chaplain. Then there are the clerks of the House who know most about the place, who are professionals, and so are the attendants and the police. Then there is the Prime Minister and his Ministers and the Leader of the Opposition—all professionals. Mr Gardner is a barrister and appears before the judges as a professional before professionals. Is there any 'discord in the spirit, tradition and history' of the Law Courts because the judges are full-time employees of the Crown? The House of Lords is full of professionals too, from the Lord Chancellor and the Archbishop of Canterbury down, and there are the pensioned-off professionals.

At the apex of our constitution is the Queen. Of course the Queen is a professional and so is the Duke of Edinburgh and most of the Royal Family. The best-known exception is Lord Snowdon, who is in the way of being an amateur in the royalty profession because he is a professional photographer. When he became Lord Snowdon, Mr. Armstrong Jones became a semi-professional with an amateur status. It would be rather difficult for Mr Gardner to classify him.

So Mr Gardner is not on good grounds when he objects to professionalism in politics and in government. Mr Gardner put it this way:

'The right of a parliamentary candidate to financial independence from outside work is clear. What he does as a candidate for a legitimate living outside politics is his own business. But what happens once he is elected as an M.P.? Should he be compelled to give up the financial independence of his previous work, rely on his parliamentary salary and devote all his time to politics? Most M.P.s and most of the electorate would, I believe, answer emphatically 'No!'

When the facts are clearly explained to them it is extremely doubtful whether the majority of the electorate are so enthusiastic about the amateurs who really are trying to be professional money makers and professional politicians at the same time and getting their money both ways.

Could anything be more Pecksniffian than the assertions that the M.P. for Billericay makes in the concluding paragraph of his article.

'An M.P. with outside interests may sometimes find the demands of his work and Parliament in conflict. An M.P. without outside interests, with nothing but Parliament to rely upon for the support of himself and his family, may be far worse off, whatever his parliamentary salary. He could find himself having to choose between his conscience and financial ruin.

'Professional politicians are always in peril of becoming obsessed with the power of politics, with their own importance and the belief that the centre of wisdom and the world is Westminster. It is a delusion that has brought man politician and government to grief. It is a peril best avoided by serving on the back benches of all parties the status of the amat .'

One can only pose as an a eur in politics if one is prepared to neglect and desert Wes inster and leave the day-to-day work there to somebody el

CHAPTER 9

WAS MICHAEL FOOT RIGHT?

What happens in the House of Commons came in for searching examination and scrutiny when the Select Committee on Procedure met in the Session of 1964-5 and I can earnestly commend the various reports that it has issued to the study of all those interested in the reform of Parliament. The Committee took evidence from the then Speaker, Sir Harry Hylton Foster, the Chairman of Ways and Means, Dr Horace King, who later became the Speaker, clerks of the House, civil servants, various professors of politics from the universities, Mr Wm. Hamilton, M.P., the Chairman of the Estimates Committee, Mr Enoch Powell and Sir Edmund Boyle, Mr John Diamond, the Chief Secretary at the Treasury, and others, and many of them submitted memoranda. The reports cover various subjects but the one that attracted most attention among parliamentarians was the one that dealt with the question of how the extension of the Committee system might be used to provide greater information for M.P.s and improve the efficiency of Parliament.

There were widely different opinions of how this could be done and there were majority and minority recommendations. The recommendations were lengthy and difficult to summarize but the key to the majority view was contained in the final paragraph 16 which read:

(i) That a new Select Committee be set up, as a development of the present Estimates Committee, 'to examine how the departments of state carry out their responsibilities and to consider their Estimates of Expenditure and Reports'.

(ii) That the new Committee should function through Sub-Committees specializing in the various spheres of governmental activity.

(iii) That there should be two Clerks supervising the work of the Committee and one full-time Clerk to each Sub-Committee. The Committee should be able to employ specialist assistance.

(iv) That the power of Select Committees to adjourn from place to place should include the power to travel abroad, with the leave of the House, when investigations require it.

In these cautious words the Select Committee opened the door, even if only slightly, at which many people interested in parliamentary reform had been politely knocking for many years.

The question that they had been asking was whether there should not be an extension of the Committee system so that M.P.s not in the Government might get greater information and control over the Public Departments, or whether or not we should adopt in some form or another the Committee system of government which prevails in other countries and in our own local government. The Select Committee did not survey the whole range of argument but starting with the Estimates Committee looked at the question as to whether the activities of the Committee could not be enlarged and extended.

Let us then start with the Estimates Committee which was so frequently mentioned in the discussions.

The Estimates Committee was set up originally because the House of Commons thought that the enormous annual sums of Government expenditure deserved more careful consideration than was possible on the floor of the House.

Every year it meets and divides itself into Sub-Committees which have powers to examine some specific expenditure which the Committee thinks is necessary.

During recent years the Estimates Committee has investigated and reported on a very large variety of subjects. They include expenditure incurred by the Foreign Office, the Defence Services, the Health Services, the Home Office, Agriculture and many others. The Estimates Committee brings before it the civil servants and examines them at considerable length and then reports to the House.

Then the Departments which have been investigated and criticized have the right to give their observations and reply to the criticisms and then it is for Parliament to take the necessary action if any.

It cannot be doubted that during recent years the Estimates Committee has done exceedingly useful service in drawing attention to matters of considerable importance that would otherwise have been overlooked and remained unnoticed.

But the Estimates Committee can only investigate expenditure which has been approved and sanctioned. It has no power to investigate and analyze expenditure before it has been made nor the policies which have justified it.

For example, the Estimates Committee has a right to examine the expenditure incurred in establishing a nuclear submarine base at the Gareloch in Scotland. It has no power to go into the question of whether the expenditure is necessary or whether the project is desirable. This has already been decided on by the Government and approved of by the House. The Estimates Committee is not, say, like a committee of a local authority which takes an estimate of the cost of a slaughter house and whether it is desirable or necessary before beginning it. Nor is the Estimates Committee like the Finance Committee of a local authority which prepares its Budget before recommending what the ~~tes~~ should be.

Its function is to examine afterwards and that is its weakn .
It can only go and look over the stable after the horse has go~~i~~

It was Mr W. Hamilton, M.P., the Chairman of the Estimate Committee, who when the Select Committee's Report wa~~:~~ debated in the House pointed out the limitations of the Committee and the handicaps under which it worked. He said:

'The much more fundamental problem, and one which seems to me to get at the basic causes of the undoubted decline in the public esteem and prestige of Parliament, is, to quote paragraph 2 of the Fourth Report: "The question of the detailed examination of the Estimates in the broadest sense . . . " The House of Commons spends about one-third of its time discussing financial matters, but although it does that it has long since contracted out of any attempt at a detailed and comprehensive scrutiny of Estimates put before it by the Government—even in the narrowest sense. As a watchdog over public expenditure, the House of Commons has neither bark nor bite. Year after year the Government get all their way with all their Estimates. We can investigate in the Estimates Committee or on the floor of the House, but year by year the Government get all their way. Not only that, but they can deceive the House quite easily by concealing details of expenditure. We had the example of Mr Attlee spending £100 million on the atom bomb, and no one in this House knew.'

The illustration of the atom bomb shows how expenditure can be incurred without the House of Commons knowing anything about it. It was not only the £100 million on the bomb, it was the step that was taken without the House of Commons knowing what further astronomical expenditure in the years that followed that we were committed to with only the vaguest idea of what this implied.

Mr Hamilton went on to show how Parliament's powers to examine public expenditure had been reduced since the war, although this expenditure had increased from £700,000,000 in 1938 and 1939 to approximately £7,000,000,000 in 1965.

'Such control of this vast expenditure as now exists resides, not in this House but in the Treasury and, more importantly, with the Cabinet in the making of policy decisions. It is those policy decisions that determine the long-term commitments, and it is just in this field of policy making that the elected representatives have no effective control. . . . So, far from this House controlling expenditure, there is pressure from it to increase it, and the people who control it are the Executive; in other words the Treasury and above all, the Cabinet. These policy decisions are taken by the Government without any scrutiny in depth by the House, and with little consultation with the House. Parliament is very often the very last body to be consulted. Consultations are held with the TUC, with Service chiefs, with local authority organizations and with the Employers' Confederation. After that, the Government come to the House and say, "That is the policy". Then we have a debate and the whips are on because the Government regard every major debate as a vote of confidence, and they get their way. Ministers read their carefully prepared briefs, hon. Members read their carefully prepared speeches, the vote is taken, and then we move on to the next debate.

'That seems to me to point to the fact that, as at present constituted and with its existing procedures, the House is too big an assembly with too little time and not enough information to present any effective or detailed challenge to the Government. That challenge is coming, but what is a disturbing feature, in my view, is that it is coming not from the House of Commons but from the TV interviewer and the journalist. They can question Ministers uninhibited by any restrictive terms of reference and in full view of millions of electors. I believe that Ministers are often more afraid of Mr Robin Day than of any Member of the House. We are in danger of getting to a situation in which true democracy begins and ends on polling day, and thereafter the Government become virtual dictators. The Prime Minister, with access to all the facts on any given problem and possessed of enormous powers of patronage with which he can buy the silence of his most garrulous and dangerous critics, becomes almost unassailable.'

Mr Hamilton pointed out the difficulties under which the Committee (over which he presided) worked.

'As the Estimates Committee is at present constituted, with its existing terms of reference, it does a useful job, although its usefulness has tended to be exaggerated from time to time. But it labours under very considerable handicaps. The Select Committee's recommendations will go some way towards removing or at least reducing those handicaps, and, although I was not glad about very much of my right hon. Friend's speech, I was glad that he said we could go ahead with providing additional staff. I am not sure where we will get them, because recruitment problems are quite serious. If we can get two Clerks instead of one supervising the Committee as a whole and if we can get one full-time Clerk for each of the Sub-Committees and can employ specialist assistants, then these recommendations which have been accepted by the Government will go some way towards solving a number of our problems.

'I would like an assurance from my right hon. Friend that that is being looked into carefully and that the recent economy circular that has gone round to all Government Departments, including the Department of the Clerk of the House, will not adversely affect the possibility of getting those additional Clerks.

'The employment of specialist assistants will certainly not make the Estimates Committee a serious rival in any field of expertise to any Government Department; nor would we expect it to do so. We would not pretend to be on a basis of equality in that regard. But it will make the Committee less easy prey to the civil servant giving evidence, especially a civil servant from a technical department.'

Mr Hamilton pointed out that there was nothing very revolutionary in the mild recommendations of the Select Committee. It was a step towards giving Members more information about the facts which were the background of the issues which they debated.

But the indictment that he had made of the way the House of Commons worked was a formidable one.

A completely different point of view of the extension of the Committee system was taken by Mr Michael Foot, who rather surprisingly found himself in alliance with the ex-Tory Chief Whip, Sir Martin Redmayne, who voted for Mr Foot's recommendation submitted to the Committee which was rejected by nine votes to two. It read:

'Your Committee have spent long hours examining the operation of Select Committees and Supply procedure. They have, on the evidence presented to them, concluded that there are several useful reforms, within the framework of the present system, which should be adopted. However, they have been deterred from listing these at the present stage by the consideration of one major issue of principle. One proposal canvassed in many quarters and presented to them by many authorities as a major means of reforming parliamentary procedure is that a series of specialist committees should be established to examine or help formulate the general range of administration or policy. Your Committee are convinced that this idea is a delusion. Indeed, they conclude that the proliferation of parliamentary committees is not a cure but part of the disease. And they are persuaded that concentration on this issue can block or postpone a whole series of reforms which are much more urgent, practicable and desirable. Your Committee are convinced that a main purpose of parliamentary reform must be to restore the authority of the House of Commons chamber itself. For this purpose, measures should be taken to instil spontaneity and flexibility into its proceedings, and to enable debates to be held over a much wider range and at much shorter notice than is possible under present arthritic procedures. Moves in this direction could only be made more difficult by the establishment of a fresh crop of specialist committees, even if they were skilfully camouflaged as extensions of existing committees such as the Estimates Committee. More and more committees sitting while the House of Commons itself is in session can only mean that fewer and fewer Members will be available to attend its cloistered rites. Moreover, more "Committees upstairs" are likely to nurture the miserable deception that more and more issues can profitably be "taken out of politics". On the contrary, the purpose of parliamentary reform should be to take more issues into politics, into Parliament, and, above all, into Parliament's principal place of debate. Once this is accepted as the major principle which should govern its investigations, your Committee are convinced that a series of reforms designed to apply the principle in practice could be swiftly developed.'

Mr Foot clearly believed that Parliament badly needed reforming but his recommendation did not outline at any great length the way he would do it.

It would have been interesting if he had submitted a detailed memorandum to the Committee and been questioned about it.

He defended his views in the debate in the House but this did not carry us much further.

Mr Hamilton rather tartly remarked that he never thought that Mr Foot 'would be so terrified of a mouse', for that was all that the Committee's recommendation meant. Far from threatening the authority of the House of Commons the proposition was designed to enhance the prestige of the House and not to

CHAPTER 10

THE INEVITABLE TORY SPLIT

Between 1951 and 1964 the House of Commons several times discussed its procedure, set up a Select Committee to discuss it and then did nothing about it. The House of Commons as it existed was good enough for the Tories. When the big landlord and capitalist vested interests wanted any legislation they got it. Tory Governments pushed through the Rent Act; agricultural legislation to help the big landlords, the brewers, the gambling vested interest and anything else that those who financed the Tory Party election campaigns wanted.

Why should the Tories want any reform of Parliament? It suited them admirably. Why should they want a House of Commons that unduly interfered with Big Business or inquired too closely into its operations? A Parliament that opened its proceedings at 30 in the afternoon suited them. The last thing they wanted was an active, inquisitive House of Commons taking an active interest in affairs and determined to assert itself. They objected to planning on principle and as an interference with private enterprise. In Parliament they might carry on the delusion that they ruled the country as long as the real power remained in the board rooms of the City.

And this attitude was reflected in the outlook of the Tories when the Select Committee of Procedure of 1964 took its evidence.

The two Conservative ex-Ministers who gave evidence were Mr Enoch Powell and Sir Edward Boyle. They had rather different points of view and they were probably chosen because they had been at the Treasury.

Sir Edward Boyle is regarded at Westminster as one of the more progressive Tories. He resigned over Suez, he had more enlightened views on education than some of his colleagues. On the other hand Mr Enoch Powell is known as an extreme diehard Right Wing Tory not believing in any of the new-fangled ideas about planning or an incomes and prices policy and believing as far as possible in no State interference with private capitalism. Reform of the House of Commons was obviously not one of Mr Enoch Powell's lines and he indicated this quite decisively in his evidence before the Committee.

Indeed Sir Edward Boyle found it necessary to dissociate himself from his colleague after Mr Powell had bluntly expressed the view, 'I do not think science should be debated at all in the House of Commons'. In his day Mr Gladstone had said very much the same thing about unemployment which he thought too was not a problem with which Parliament should be concerned.

Sir Edward Boyle made it clear that he could not agree with this when he said:

'I believe that the time has now come when a specialist Committee on science would prove of value. The one point my friend and colleague Mr Powell has made with which I entirely differ is his suggestion that we should never discuss science on the floor of the House.'

Now this was obviously a fundamental point of difference and showed two very different outlooks. It is a pity that Mr Powell did not explain his views at greater length, but nobody seemed to follow up his statement, probably because the members of the Committee were so completely stupefied. What exactly did Mr Powell mean when he asserted that science should be the obscene subject that should not be discussed in the House of Commons? If he had said 'sex' one could have understood it. But 'science'! One cannot imagine that the House of Commons would get very far in discussing anything if science is to be ruled out. Why, science was even mentioned in the Conservative General Election Manifesto and Mr Quintin Hogg had special ministerial responsibilities for it in the Conservative Government. After the Election Mr Powell was appointed the Conservative Shadow Minister for Defence. Whether it was because of this remark one does not know. How Parliament can discuss nuclear strategy and modern weapons in a Defence debate if Mr Powell flatly refused to discuss science on the floor of the House is not clear as I write.

Certainly his view staggered Sir Edward Boyle. If we are not to discuss science on the floor of the House of Commons in the year 1966 we might as well shut the place up, which is a proposition that Mr Powell might agree with.

No wonder that the proposal for setting up more specialized Committees found no favour with him.

He said in reply to a further question he was asked later:

'I am as deeply suspicious of the idea of "specialized" Members as I am of the idea of 'specialized' Ministers. I believe it is our business, whether on the back or front benches, not to be specialists and not to be identifiable in the sense of being held to be expert in a particular subject. I should deplore anything which resulted in a cadre of foreign affairs Members or social service Members coming into existence. No doubt Members will wish to interest themselves first in one subject and then in another, but that is a very different matter.'

But Members of Parliament do already specialize in various subjects. Indeed if Mr Powell ever becomes the Minister of Defence in a Conservative Government he will have to be the supreme specialist. His argument was not one against specialized Committees but against the specialized Committees always consisting of the same members, which nobody has ever suggested.

Another objection that Mr Powell raised to having the Estimates Committee increased in membership so that it could have special Committees for special Ministers was:

'The work of the Estimates Committee is a very heavy burden, if it is properly done, and the members of it and I feel there is a limit in the number of Members who are available to do that work at the required standard.'

If this criticism is right then the House of Commons must be a poor place indeed. This indicates that Mr Powell is sceptical of the quality of Conservative Members because he can have little knowledge of the capacity, experience, and ability of the newly-elected Labour Members.

If the House of Commons, out of its membership of 630, could not supply say fifty Members to undertake the task of scrutinizing in detail the way national money is being spent then indeed it is very devoid of people who were elected precisely because the electors thought they were capable of doing the job. Indeed Mr Powell must have a poor opinion of the members of his own party. If they are incapable of being on the Estimates Committee how can they be capable of being directors of the various companies with which they are associated?

On the other hand if the argument is that the Tory Party has sufficient Members to work on Committees if they were not employed elsewhere then it is obvious that they are putting their own private interests before that of the country and should not be in Parliament at all.

Sir Edward Boyle put his point of view on the case for specialist Committees as follows:

'On the subject of specialized Committees generally, I should not want to see these rapidly increase in number at any one time. I think we should go slowly. However, despite the misgivings of some people the Select Committee on Nationalized Industries has proved a success. It is relevant here that the report on transport has been widely studied at the universities. Indeed the Stationery Office was remiss at one time in not having enough copies of this report available. I believe that the time has come when a specialist Committee on science would prove of value.'

Nobody who knows Westminster believes that it is possible to appoint specialist Committees for every Government Department overnight. That would indeed be a major political revolution. But one welcomes Sir Edward Boyle's statement as indicating that some move should be made, even at tortoise speed, in contrast to Mr Powell's view that there should be no movement at all.

What convinced Sir Edward Boyle that a new approach was justified was the work of the Select Committee on Nationalized Industries which has published a number of very useful reports.

The Conservatives were quite prepared to have the nationalized industries investigated ad lib in the hope that they would find mistakes and inefficiency which would be used as propaganda against further nationalization.

Now if it is desirable to have periodical investigations into nationalized industries why not similar inquiries into groups of non-nationalized industries?

If Sir Edward Boyle were to venture to ask a question like this the odds are that he would be expelled from the Conservative Party tomorrow. Yet surely other key British industries require to be investigated too. If London Transport, why not shipping and shipbuilding? As I write the Government has just put up

£1,000,000 to keep the Fairfield Shipbuilding Company going while its affairs are being examined by the Official Receiver. If the Government is to subsidise why should it not investigate and get all the facts. Sir Edward Boyle could only agree to this over Mr Enoch Powell's dead body. What would be next? Would it be the machine tools industry or Imperial Chemicals or even the banks and the insurance companies.

Mr Enoch Powell is logical enough. He wants no, or as little interference as possible with the operations of private capitalism.

One wonders not why Mr Enoch Powell is against modernizing Parliament but why he is in favour of Parliament at all. The difference between Sir Edward Boyle and Mr Powell is not just limited to the argument as to whether or not we should have more committees in Parliament. Sir Edward Boyle wants the Conservatives to realize that we must discuss science in the House of Commons. We are in 1966. But Mr Powell is not in favour of 1966. He is still in 1866 and wants Parliament to meddle as little with private capitalism as it did then.

There are of course more Tory M.P.s in favour of Mr Powell than the fifteen who voted for him in his bid for the leadership of the Tory Party. Personally I regret that he did not get it. With Mr Powell you would at least know where you were, just as you knew where you were with Sir Alec Douglas Home. Nobody doubted the political honesty of Sir Alec. But the Conservative Party had to remove him from the centre of the political stage because he was obviously the medieval landlord and Eton and Oxford and all that. Fundamentally Sir Alec was a far better representative leader of British Conservatism than Mr Heath. Mr Enoch Powell refused to join up in Sir Alec's Government because he thought he was too revolutionary and one can honour him for that. It remains to be seen whether the Conservative Party did the wisest thing by politely assassinating Sir Alec Douglas Home or by rejecting Mr Enoch Powell.

It chose Mr Heath largely because they thought he would be a better swashbuckler in the political pillow fighting in the House of Commons and because he would be a better salesman for an alleged new Conservative policy over TV. As it turned out he was knocked about so easily by Harold Wilson in Parliament that the fifteen Powellites were soon able to say 'I told you so' and others were able to say 'Don't blame me. I voted Maudling'.

The new Conservative leader wasn't the greatly expected success on TV either. The public were not quite certain whether he was trying to sell them a new Conservative policy or a new toothpaste.

Indeed, if what the Tory Party needed most was someone who could successfully go on the TV and sell the Conservative Party and its ideas as the professional advertising expert hopes to sell a new toothpaste Mr Heath was certainly their man and not Mr Enoch Powell. Had Mr Enoch Powell been chosen to sell a toothpaste on the television he would have stuck to his script until the last minute and then thrown it away and said 'No, I have come to the conclusion that this toothpaste is a fraud. Don't buy it! I resign.' But if Mr Heath were employed he would have gone through it to the end, though one doubts whether there would be a rush to buy the toothpaste next day.

Mr Enoch Powell is a very good debater, much better than Mr Heath, but he is not such a good salesman. But he is the most interesting personality on the Tory side. He would have been quite at home in the Roundhead Parliament and he would have been a hundred per cent behind Oliver Cromwell for the beheading of the King and later would have been hung, drawn and quartered for regicide. When I first heard him speak in the House I realized that the real fanatic had arrived. His place was not on the Tory benches at all. Indeed he ought to be provided with a bench of his own. Certainly his place is not on the Tory Front Bench. Almost as soon as he got on to the Government Front Bench he resigned. Then he retired to the back benches again when Sir Alec Douglas Home became Prime Minister. Sir Alec was too advanced for him. 'The trouble about Enoch', said a Tory M.P. to me, 'is that he resigns too often. One never quite knows when he is going to do it next.' Enoch Powell was certainly the strangest apparition that appeared on the Tory Front Bench when Mr Heath became the new Leader. He was to be the new Shadow Minister for Defence! I cannot imagine Mr Enoch Powell becoming a real Minister of Defence but if he does I cannot imagine him being there very long for he thinks too much. His demand that the Tory Party should reconsider whether we should go on spending more money on an East of

Suez policy was certainly a strange idea to come from the Tory Front Bench or any Tory bench and was promptly repudiated. Yet he coupled this with an emotional appeal to retain the Territorials, at a cost of £20,000,000 a year, although what the Territorials can do in the event of an explosion of a megaton bomb over Britain, except to prepare for the Resurrection, nobody knows. I cannot remember any similar speech in recent political history in which such a mixture of realism and romanticism got mixed up in the same speech. Yet the Tory Party Conference, when he had presented it, gave him a standing ovation which must have been the first occasion in history when it had become enthusiastic and almost delirious about an obvious anarchist. For Mr Enoch Powell is a confessed anarchist and he looks like one. He has the detached, mysterious air of the cloak-and-dagger conspirator. An anarchist is against planning of any kind. So is Mr Powell. He has attacked the Conservative Party because it has gone so far in agreeing with Socialist ideas of planning. The Conservatives no longer regard planning as a dirty word. Mr Macmillan in one of his last speeches in Parliament was quite enthusiastic about it. Not so Mr Powell. In his book A Nation Not Afraid, the Thinking of Enoch Powell, there is a chapter on 'Planning the Economy' which begins with the sentences:

'One of the worst traps for the free society was sprung by the Conservatives. It may seem a little exaggerated to describe the N.E.D.C. (the National Economic Development Council, 'Neddy') in this way, but there is no doubt that the ideas behind it reflect many of the fallacies of Socialism, in particular the claim to be able to foresee and provide for the future, which in turn rests on the claim to be able to select those industries which should expand and (presumably) those which should contract. Implicit in the whole approach is the assumption that a decision made in Whitehall is likely to be superior to one made elsewhere.'

One wonders what would happen at the Ministry of Defence if Mr Powell arrived there and proceeded to put these theories into practice. There would soon arrive a situation in which if Mr Powell did not again resign the rest of the Cabinet would.
Further on we are told:

'It is remarkable that Labour's design to plan individual industries should have been anticipated by the Conservative administration. It was, after all, the Tories who brought nine little Neddies into being. Mr Powell called them "the little Trojan horses".'

Mr Powell is so emphatically against planning that one is justified in placing him among the anarchists. The Defence chiefs would recommend him as a Trojan horse immediately he arrived.

When we turn to the chapter on 'Incomes Policy v. Inflation' we are told:

'About the same time that the Conservative Party fell for planning economic growth it found itself drawn into the attempt to plan incomes (an "incomes policy").'

This was under Mr Macmillan and Mr Heath supported it. Mr Enoch Powell is quite capable of springing surprises on his Conservative friends. In his chapter on trade unions he expresses the view that 'the shop steward in general suffers an unduly bad press' and that he is 'a widely misunderstood and therefore unfairly abused phenomenon' which is rather a curious description of a shop steward.

Mr Powell has a capacity for candour which can often upset the Conservative apple cart.

'There is a prevalent superstition,' he writes, 'that the British economy is plagued with strikes. This superstition is ill founded. Britain is nowhere at the top of the international league of days lost by strikes in proportion to the size of the labour force.'

This superstition is so generally accepted by the Conservatives in Parliament that Mr Powell did a service by exploding it.

These surprisingly progressive deviations from his general line do not however hide the fact that Mr Powell represents the extreme Conservative Right while Sir Edward Boyle, who appeared with him to give evidence at the Procedure Committee, is generally supposed to be on the Conservative Left. These are two distinct trends which Mr Heath will have difficulty in harmonizing and with all his experience in the handling of choirs he will have trouble in getting the Powells and the Boyles to sing in tune.

I shall always associate Sir Edward Boyle with the occasion when as Minister of Education he was presenting some Bill or other and had to do the conventional marching and bowing from the Bar to the Table of the House.

He did it very timidly and self-consciously, like a rather well fed tabby cat, tripping gingerly on a very doubtful tightrope. As he advanced one heard Sir Gerald Nabarro's deep sergeant-major voice boom out 'Keep it in, man! Keep it in!', which was not a reference to the motion that Sir Edward was introducing.

One doubts if Sir Gerald Nabarro will be one of Sir Edward Boyle's backers should Mr Heath retire. He has no time for progressive Tories either.

Only a few Tories favour the modernization of Parliament. The majority do not.

Not that they will refuse to make unsympathetic noises and profess interest in the need for reform. The greatest expert and Leader of the House at making sympathetic noises which meant nothing was Mr R. A. Butler. That was the reason why he thought he was the ideal man to make Master of Trinity College, Cambridge. Mr Butler was always prepared to let the Committee of Procedure discuss Parliamentary reform provided that in the last resort it did nothing about it.

The City quite rightly looks at Westminster as its natural enemy.

In a pamphlet called *Change or Decay* published in 1963 a group of Conservative M.P.s under the chairmanship of Sir William Robson Brown had urged that the Committee Stage of the Finance Bill should be taken upstairs.

They said:

'The Bill, despite its enormous importance for the country's trade and standard of living, is often debated in a manner which is frustrating to the Member who is not an expert on taxation. The discussions are carried on by not more Members than could easily sit in a large Standing Committee.

'The remainder, however, are not spared for other duties. On the contrary they must remain always available, ready to leap instantly at the sound of the division bell. For there may be numerous divisions from 3.30 p.m. onwards (when other work in the House of

Commons is necessarily interrupted) and all Members who are not "paired" have to file through the Lobby. It is not generally realized that five divisions take up one hour.

'Is this sort of thing really necessary in modern times? The Select Committee on Procedure of 1958-9 said that it was not and that tradition ought not to stand in the way of reform. They recommended that part or parts of the Finance Bill be committed to Standing Committees. This has not been done and the Finance Bill still remains on the floor of the House in its Committee stage a time-wasting operation for all but those interested in the technicalities of particular clauses and amendments, consuming, as it invariably does, the major share of parliamentary time during the summer session.

'This is the sort of thing which makes the House of Commons appear, in the eyes of industry and the country. as a whole unbusinesslike . . . What little is known outside Parliament about its procedures and the duties of its Members gives the impression of a clumsy and traditional system. Members, for example, attend for long hours when little constructive work can be done. To many this type of public service looks increasingly unattractive. Reports of sittings in the early hours of the morning have in recent times done much to damage the prestige of the House of Commons as an efficient legislative, although they are entirely in keeping with the principles of democracy. At the end of the past summer an important Minister of the Crown wound up a debate at 6 a.m. after a sitting of some sixteen hours. An hour later he was obliged to fly to a public engagement in the North of England. . . . If a serious attempt was made to reform the procedure of the House of Commons many of these problems might be overcome, and the status of Parliament and its Members enhanced.'

But no serious attempt was made by the Conservative Government to do anything about it. If it was to be a choice between change and decay it preferred decay. That, however, was no reason why a Labour Government should do the same.

CHAPTER 11

HAVE PRIME MINISTERS TOO MUCH POWER?

Among the witnesses who gave evidence before the Committee of Procedure was Dr Horace King, who was then Deputy Speaker and Chairman of Ways and Means, and later, following the death of Sir Harry Hylton-Foster, became the Speaker.

His evidence was mainly concerned with House of Commons procedure in relation to finance.

Dr King is the first Labour Speaker and so his views are interesting as expressing the outlook of a Speaker who is not a lawyer, was not a front bencher and who had sat on the back benches as an ordinary M.P.

He began by saying: 'I would say, first of all, that I am a traditionalist and I make no apologies for saying that. It is part of my function as Chairman of Ways and Means to guard the traditions of the House'.

But he immediately qualified this by saying: 'If tradition stands in the way of efficiency, then I would ask that tradition go; but if tradition does not stand in the way of efficiency then I would say that I would ask the Committee to recommend that it stay'.

So that the stress was on the word efficiency, which was all to the good. Nobody can object to Dr King being a traditionalist if efficiency comes first, although one would also add that if the traditions serve no useful purpose and do not improve the usefulness of Parliament there is a case for giving a critical and irreverent look at them too.

He urged the Committee 'when making its recommendations to see that it does not throw the baby out with the bath water'. All this might have been necessary advice to give to that not very revolutionary body, the Select Committee of Procedure, although the throwing out of babies with the bath water is not one of the most regular habits of the British people and hardly one of our cherished traditions. He reminded the Committee that 'the traditions of Parliament are part of the glories of Parliament'. Now nobody who has been in Parliament for any length of time has failed to hear this reference to 'the glories of Parliament' which is one of the conventional stock-in-trade platitudes of the place. I have so often heard so many different speakers say the same thing, although by it they don't mean the same thing, if they mean anything.

There is by no means unanimity about what have been the glories of Parliament and what have been not. Some hold the opinion that the most glorious episode in the history of Parliament was when it cut off the King's head, while others hold the view that the glorious moment was the Restoration when Parliament made regicide a crime and cut off the heads of those who had cut off the King's head.

One can concede that all institutions have had their glorious moments of a kind, but their history is not a history of a succession of glorious moments.

Nobody who knows anything about the history of Parliament can be ignorant of the fact that it has had its inglorious moments too and that a lot of dirty work has been done there as well. There were times when Parliament revolted against the King but there were the times when Parliament licked the King's boots too. There were the times when Parliament was absolutely corrupt and times when it was callous and cruel, servile, ignorant and incompetent.

Taking a cool look at it there is precious little reason why we should be mesmerised and hypnotised by the glories of Parliament so as to forget that it is far from being the most perfect institution in the world yet.

When Dr King went on to remark 'I am one of those who think that the power of the Executive is growing and that it ought to be diminished' he was on more solid ground and one hopes that he will continue to act on this assumption during his period of Speakership. But it is the House of Commons itself that will be to blame and not the Speaker if it allows the Executive to take its powers from it.

Nobody can deny that during the war Britain remained formally a democracy, but the powers vested in Winston Churchill were very much those of a dictator. True the House of Commons met regularly and the Prime Minister made regular orations there, but immense powers were vested in the War Cabinet which Churchill dominated. This position changed during the years that Attlee was Prime Minister between 1945 and 1951. He was not such a forceful and formidable personality as Churchill and one would not describe him as a dictator Prime Minister. Besides, he had powerful personalities in his Cabinet who would not have tolerated from Attlee what the war-time Cabinet had tolerated from Churchill. Cripps, Dalton, Morrison, Bevan—to name only a few—were as forceful personalities as Attlee and there was intrigue against him. If Attlee did have enormous power as Prime Minister he had to use it judiciously and with discretion.

When Churchill returned to power after the General Election of 1951 he was ageing and he was not so interested in peace as he was in war so he was content to relax his grip and leave matters more to his Ministers.

Anthony Eden was not long enough in office to acquire the prestige of a dictator and one does not look back on him as one either.

But Harold Macmillan in his later years of office definitely assumed the role of the ruthless political dictator working within the background of our parliamentary system.

The Prime Minister can change his Cabinet at will and this gives him enormous powers. When Harold Macmillan was faced in July 1962 with the undeniable fact that his Government was unpopular and that the next General Election would mean the defeat of his Government he ruthlessly sacked seven of his Cabinet colleagues. The *Daily Telegraph* called the great purge of July 1962 'the most sweeping Government reconstruction in modern times'. Overnight the Prime Minister sacked seven of his Cabinet Ministers. They were the Lord Chancellor, the Chancellor of the Exchequer, the Minister of Defence, the Minister of Education, the Minister of Housing and Lord Mills, Minister without portfolio, one of the Government's chief spokesmen in the House of Lords.

When I heard this news over the wireless I asked myself the question which I have never seen satisfactorily answered, why one man should have had the power to do this in a democracy. They were by no means the most conspicuous failures in the

Government. Macmillan had himself presumably chosen them for their political abilities and they had been no more failures at the dispatch box than the others. Why these Ministers had been specially singled out for dismissal has never been clearly explained.

In his memoirs, *Political Adventure*, the Earl of Kilmuir lifts the veil a little. He tells us:

'None of us thought that the months ahead were going to be easy, but there was a general feeling of relief that after months of dithering we knew where we were going.

'Nevertheless, inside the Government as well as outside, no one could ignore the fact that the appalling series of by-election disasters showed no sign of abatement. On Monday, July 9th, the Central Office warned the Prime Minister that another humiliation was inevitable in the pending North-East Leicester by-election. This was a highly marginal seat, with a Labour majority of only 1,431 over the Conservatives. On Tuesday, July 10th, Sylvia (Lady Kilmuir) was talking to Macmillan at a State banquet. He murmured to her, "I have the most terrible problems on my mind", but she naturally assumed that he was referring to the unusual but not really abnormal number of difficult matters facing the Government.

'On the following evening, as a meeting of a Committee of the Cabinet was ending, Macmillan took me aside and said, "The Government is breaking up", and murmured something about "You don't mind going?" I was startled but merely replied, "You know my views".'

There was obviously no question of Lord Kilmuir having not done his duty and served the Macmillan Government well in the House of Lords. For Macmillan had told Lord Kilmuir not to go abroad in September because he needed him for the important Commonwealth Prime Ministers' Conference and for the anticipated Common Market negotiations the following year.

The morning after the result of the Leicester by-election, where Labour retained the seat with a slightly increased majority, Lord Kilmuir was attending another Committee of the Cabinet when he was handed a message that the Prime Minister wished to see him.

Lord Kilmuir tells us:

'Our interview began at 11.15 and lasted about three-quarters of an hour. What was said must remain confidential, but the results are well known. Seven Cabinet Ministers were to go, and there was to be a corresponding shake-up among junior Ministers, and the reconstruction was to be immediate and dramatic. I got the impression that he was extremely alarmed about his own position, and was determined to eliminate any risk for himself by a massive change of Government. It astonished me that a man who had kept his head under the most severe stresses and strains should lose both nerve and judgment in this way.

'I once remarked to a young historian that "loyalty was the Tories' secret weapon". I doubt if it has ever had to endure so severe a strain.'

After leaving the Prime Minister, Lord Kilmuir had seven hours of office left. When he listened to the wireless that night he learned he had been sacked and had been made an earl.

Lord Kilmuir describes the incident with great restraint. But what must he and the other Ministers have thought about this amazing incident. A Lord Chancellor, the head of the House of Lords and the British legal system, was sacked from the Woolsack with less notice than would have been given to one of the cleaners in the House of Lords.

When one read that Sir Reginald Manningham Buller was to become Lord Dilhorne and succeed to the Lord Chancellorship one could only gasp with incredulity.

In the Commons Kilmuir had been a far more capable lawyer stonewalling for the Government in an awkward situation than ever his successor had been. I never heard any convincing reason given at the time why Lord Dilhorne had been chosen to succeed Lord Kilmuir. The only reason that was advanced was that Macmillan at some time or other had promised the Attorney General promotion, exactly why was not clear to those who had sat on the benches when he performed at the dispatch box. Indeed if the Lord Chancellor's job had been advertised one doubted whether Sir Reginald would have been on the short list. There was also considerable sympathy at the time for Mr Selwyn Lloyd. He had served Macmillan faithfully and well, carrying out Macmillan's foreign policy and also his financial policy as Chancellor of the Exchequer. I was in Moscow at the time of the famous Macmillan mission in 1957 and everybody took it for granted that Selwyn Lloyd was just playing the part of the monkey while Macmillan was the organ grinder. Because the tunes that Macmillan was grinding out on his organ were no longer popular he tried to reverse his misfortunes by discarding the monkey.

G

Even the Foreign Secretary, Sir Alec Douglas Home, was not sure that day whether he was for the chopper or not. Mr Robert Edwards, M.P., has told me that, along with Mr Arthur Woodburn, he was in the Foreign Office that fateful day when Lord Home, as he then was, came in. When they congratulated him upon still being Foreign Secretary he replied, 'I don't know yet, there may be a letter on my desk'.

No Scots M.P. could understand why John Maclay, with his considerable experience of business in Scotland and his conscientiousness and hard work at the Scottish Office, had been forced to resign in favour of Mr Michael Noble, the Argyllshire sheep farmer who had no experience of the Scottish Office as an under secretary but had merely been a junior whip. Nobody could seriously argue that from the point of view of ability the new Ministers were any better than the old ones. Indeed the new ones were in most cases worse. Many of the sacked ones were soon given important jobs in the City, some of them with better salaries. The only reason that was given was that the by-elections were showing that the country wanted to see changes in the Government and that a newly reconstructed Government would enable Macmillan to convince the country at the General Election that a new Government had been formed. Nemesis, however, overtook Macmillan and he was not to fulfil his promise to the Young Conservatives that he would again lead them to victory and he finally dished Butler and bequeathed the Tory Party a new leader in Sir Alec Douglas Home, which was perhaps his worst disservice of all. One of the first declarations of Sir Alec was that winning the General Election for the Tory Party at the Election and not the decent government of the country was the keynote of his policy, and we know the result. The Election was put off from June to October although Macmillan had previously informed us that the uncertainty about the date of a General Election was the main reason for unemployment and so for the next six months the Tory Government kept plunging us into more and more debt.

Looking back it is impossible to resist the conclusion that Macmillan as Prime Minister had too much power. One reason was that he could threaten to hand in his resignation and call for a General Election. The Tory rank and file knew that he held this ace. The fate of every one of them was in Macmillan's hands.

Only a few Tory back benchers who had given up all hope of office, like Nigel Birch and Legge-Bourke, dared to criticize. But it was clear to every honest observer of the parliamentary scene that too much power was concentrated in the hands of the Prime Minister.

Professor Bernard Crick in his book *The Reform of Parliament* comes to the same conclusion as Dr Horace King, that the power of the Executive is increasing. He points out that in recent years the number of appointments that are at the disposal of the Prime Minister has steadily grown.

'A modern Prime Minister', he says, 'has a patronage beyond the wildest dreams of political avarice of a Walpole or a Newcastle.'

There are many more Cabinet Ministers today as compared with the number at the beginning of the century.

Between other Ministers, Ministers of State, Under Secretaries, Whips, etc. there are over 120 Members of the Government and a large number of unpaid Parliamentary Private Secretaries which altogether it is estimated make up about one half of the Parliamentary Labour Party. All these are bound to support Cabinet decisions.

So the power of the Prime Minister and the Executive is very strong indeed.

One can imagine that Harold Wilson, brought up in the democratic traditions of the Labour Party, was himself disturbed when he found what powers had been bequeathed to him by the working of our Cabinet system. Nobody in the Labour Party would dream of suggesting that the leader of the Labour Party should have the power to appoint its National Executive or half the delegates to the Annual Conference of the Labour Party. But that is how it works out in Parliament. To reduce the power of the Prime Minister would be a considerable constitutional change that could not be accomplished by any Government with a small majority, even if it desired to do so.

Has not the time come when Parliament itself should take a hand in the appointment of Ministers without leaving it entirely in the hands of the Prime Minister? No local authority would agree to its chairman having the absolute power to personally choose all the chairmen of the various committees.

Then ought we not to be asking the question whether the

Prime Minister has under our present Constitution too much power to call a General Election on his own initiative? Parliament is supposed to be elected for a five-year period. That is the legal term for which the electors choose their M.P.s. Yet Prime Ministers can plunge the country into General Elections to suit themselves. One idea worth considering is that a fifth of the Members of Parliament should stand for election every year. Members of local authorities have to be re-elected every three years. Would some such change be preferable to our present system and give us an annual election of one-fifth of the House of Commons every year? Our present system gives too much power to a Prime Minister. Parliament should be more powerful than any Prime Minister.

CHAPTER 12

PARLIAMENT AND DEFENCE

Between 1951 and 1964 successive Tory Governments spent over £20,000 million on defence and when Sir Alec Douglas Home's Government asked the House of Commons to approve the Statement on Defence (the White Paper) on February 27, 1964, Mr George Brown moved the following official Labour Party amendment declaring:

'to approve the Statement on Defence 1964 which reveals that Her Majesty's Government, in asking the taxpayer for the largest military budget in Great Britain's peace-time history, bringing its total defence expenditure over twelve years to more than £20,000 million, has still failed to produce an adequate defence policy and provide forces to meet the country's needs.'

Now £20,000 million is an enormous sum of money involving not only expenditure on the Army, Navy and the Air Force but in economic and industrial effort at home and overseas and a heavy burden on the British taxpayer. And during these years Britain was staggering along from one economic crisis to another while the nations who had lost the war, Germany and Japan, were rebuilding their basic industries in order to become our greatest industrial competitors and rivals. Those were the years too of the development of the atomic and the hydrogen bomb and its acquirement by Russia. Nobody can seriously argue that at the time when the Tory Party went out of office Britain was any safer than when it went in. On the contrary, nuclear weapons had been developed to such an extent that it was clear that if nuclear war came this country could be destroyed in a few hours. It was the age of the missile and the rocket in which old ideas about strategy and defence were no longer relevant.

Yet the arms race went on and the amount of money that Parliament voted for defence grew every year. I took part in most of the debates over the years and listened attentively to most of the speeches. Then I had opposed the Labour Government's rearmament programme which the Tories had taken over and increased and accelerated. I approached the question from the pacifist point of view, unvariably stressing the futility of the arms race, its dangers and its economic consequences. I was usually in a tiny minority which sometimes went down to one and twice my attitude led to my expulsion from the Parliamentary Labour Party. Looking back at those debates I would not contend that my arguments were always right but I can safely say that I was as right as any of the others. Of course I was invariably repudiated by the Labour Front Bench and by the Government Front Bench too. The Conservative Front Bench spokesman took over the brief that had been used when he was Minister of Defence by Mr Shinwell. It usually began by saying that when it came to discussing defence there was always the pacifist point of view which one respected but which one had to reject. So they respected and rejected me consistently over the years, the eight—or was it nine?—Ministers of Defence with always the same formula. Whether it was the same civil servant who survived to write the speeches of all the Ministers who came and went I do not know, but the theme was the same. I never expected an answer to my criticisms and never had one. Not that my criticisms of the Government's proposals were abstract or nebulous in any way. I always made a careful study of the detailed Army, Navy, Air and Civil Defence Estimates and maintained that I was taking part in the debates representing the taxpayer and the Chancellor of the Exchequer. I always argued that we were not getting the value for our money and that the taxpayers' money was going down the drain.

I was not, of course, doing anything very new. It had all been done a century before by Joseph Hume, the Radical M.P. who represented Aberdeen, and when I discovered this I was surprised how similar was the theme of our speeches. With Hume's position I cordially agreed. He used to argue that all the expenditure on defence was so much waste of the nation's money and would have been better spent on improving the condition of the people. We would be infinitely better off if we followed a foreign policy which kept us out of war.

But there was one important difference. The money that the Government asked for in Hume's day was microscopic compared with what we were spending and as a result of two world wars and the arrival of the atomic age we were much more in danger of destruction as a nation than we were then.

What seemed to me one of the most noteworthy features of the Defence and Service Estimates debate was the small number of Members that attended them, especially in view of the fact that so much money was being voted. The main reason was that for some years after 1951 the Labour Party did not divide against the Defence White Paper and when it ultimately decided to do so did not logically follow this up by voting on the various Service Estimates. The reason given for this was that this action might be misrepresented as a vote against the service men's pay. Apparently before the war the Labour Party had challenged the Estimates, and had been taunted about it, and was anxious not to be dubbed pacifist or anti-patriotic, although it could have voted against the policies contained in the Estimates by moving a token reduction of a small sum or moving a reduction by a small number of men which was the established practice of a critical Opposition.

So knowing that there was to be no vote, most Members regarded the Service Estimates days as days off, leaving the debates to be carried on by a handful on either side. In all my twenty years in Parliament I have never known the House to be so consistently empty as on these days and my summing of the proceedings with the remark that 'Never was so much money spent by so few' was amply justified. In the debate on the army, the army men turned up, on the navy day the ex-naval officers and the Members for the naval ports with their local grievances, and on the Air Estimates we had the ex-R.A.F. men and those interested in contracts for aircraft.

I once remarked that in the debate on the army, the number who listened to it could have been comfortably accommodated in a bus, on the navy day they could have been put in a small barge and on the Air Estimates day in a small Dakota aircraft.

Considering that each estimate meant approving of the expenditure of approximately £500,000,000 this showed an extraordinary lack of interest in how the nation's money was spent. All this was with the connivance of the party whips, who were not pleased when I used to try to draw the attention of the public outside to what was happening by calling frequent counts. I used to remark that it was necessary to know if the garrison was still there. Another problem for the Tory Government whips was that they had to keep forty of their Members there to prevent the House being counted out and 100 if they wished to carry the closure. I knew that Thursday night was the testing time for the Government whip for that was the time when most of the garrison disappeared. I remember in the early hours of one Friday morning, on the occasion of one of the Air Estimates debates, Mr Edward Heath, then Government whip, losing his temper completely (and he was more genial then than he is now) and hissing in my ear, 'Emrys, if there were half a dozen like you this bloody place would be simply impossible'. I replied pleasantly that I liked to see the garrison on parade.

Yet I was able to speak in almost every Service debate because there were so many ex-officers on the Conservative side who made their only speech of the year on these occasions and the Labour speakers dried up or went home so I had to be called before the end of the debate. In later years the Standing Orders were altered, which meant the debate being closed automatically at twelve o'clock, but there was hardly one debate between 1951 and 1964 that I did not make a speech with suitable variations and different figures on the theme that the taxpayer was being called upon to pay enormous sums on defence which was not defence at all.

I never flattered myself that I ever influenced anyone or cared whether I had any audience except the couple of people on the two front benches who put their feet up on the table, studying the polite and amiable platitudes that they were to interchange at the end of the debates.

I mention all this to show the background of the Estimates debates during the thirteen years of Tory rule. When George Brown complained bitterly in 1964 that £20,000 million had been spent on defence and that at the end of it there was no adequate defence I could at least murmur that they couldn't blame me.

Neither could they blame my friend Colonel George Wigg who approached the Service debates from an entirely different angle but came to conclusions with which I often entirely agreed.

During these years he was far and away the most informed and persistent critic of the Government on the Socialist back benches, an absolute encyclopaedia of information about everything relating to defence. He stoutly maintained on every possible occasion that the House was giving far too little attention to defence policy and argued that there should be a Defence Expenditure Committee, and I found his arguments unanswerable.

Were these aimless debates in the House of Commons the real way to find out about Defence Expenditure justifiable?

Before the House passed these enormous sums were we not entitled to far more detailed information than we were given in the Defence White Paper or the statistics that were thrown at us in the Service Estimates?

Wigg put the following motion on the Order Paper which would amend the Standing Orders to enable such a Committee to be set up:

Insert new *Standing Order* No. 90B (Defence Expenditure
   Committee).

There shall be a Select Committee, to be designated the Defence Expenditure Committee, to examine such of the Estimates presented to this House as are concerned with expenditure on defence either by service or civil departments, including home defence expenditure by civil departments, and to report upon the effectiveness of the policy which those Estimates are designed to implement, to consist of fifteen Members, who shall be nominated at the commencement of every session, and of whom five shall be a quorum.

The Committee shall have power to send for persons, papers and records, to sit notwithstanding any adjournment of the House, to adjourn from place to place, and to report from time to time.

It shall be at the discretion of the Committee to require every person, not being a member of the Committee, to withdraw.'

Wigg found a certain support for his proposal from a number of Conservative M.P.s who specialized in defence matters.

One of them was Mr Julian Critchley, who represented Rochester and Chatham until the General Election of 1964.

In an interesting article entitled 'Why Defence Lacks a Forum' which was published in *The Times* (3.7.65), Mr Critchley put a Conservative point of view as follows:

'Defence is not a subject in which Parliament takes much interest. There is a brief "open session", as it has been described by Mr Wigg, at the beginning of each year: two days given to the debate on the White Paper, which is the annual announcement by the Government of its defence policy, a day for each of the service estimates and perhaps another day later in the year at the request of the Opposition. Less than four per cent of parliamentary time is devoted to defence, on which has been spent since the end of the war between one quarter and a third of all Government expenditure.

'Parliament can either approve or disapprove of Government policies. It has no power, as Congress has, to reduce or increase the budget, or even to alter the pattern of allocation. The debates themselves are unrewarding. They remain very general, for Members rarely enter into the technicalities of the subject owing to the inaccessibility of "classified" and "semi-classified" information. Nor can the backbench defence committees receive secret testimony from military experts.

'Those M.P.s who would take an interest in defence are obliged to rely upon the defence correspondents of the serious press to do their "devilling" for them. It is the belief that they are inadequately informed that inhibits Members from attempting to master the financial and technical details of defence.'

Mr Critchley put his argument moderately and cautiously and in a restrained manner appropriate to the leading page of *The Times*, but it was nevertheless a formidable case against the way Parliament has been dealing with defence matters. He thought that on the whole the debates on defence in the Lords were better because of the number of prominent military personalities who were there and spoke, like Lord Montgomery, from a lifetime of experience. Mr Critchley continued :

'Parliament has been excluded from direct participation in the policy-making processes. It has had no voice in many, if not all, of the major policy decisions that have been taken since the war. Lord Attlee neither informed nor consulted Parliament before embarking on the construction of a strategic nuclear force. Nor had Parliament any say in the Conservative decision to commit conventional, and then later, nuclear, forces to the NATO alliance.

'Parliament's failure to provide a forum for defence policy has meant that no informed public opinion has been created.'

Mr Critchley's assertion that less than four per cent of parliamentary time is devoted to defence, on which has been spent since the war between one-quarter and one-third of all Government expenditure, 'that is more than £20,000 million', is a fair comment on how Parliament has been conducting its business for the last twenty years. But according to Mr Critchley the Conservative hierarchy is not anxious to change the procedure.

If the Committee which Mr Wigg advocated had been in existence during the last twenty years would we have had this enormous expenditure? The need for a Select Committee continually examining the enormous bills coming under the then Defence Expenditure was clearly indicated by Mr Robert Edwards, M.P., who was appointed the Chairman of the Sub-Committee on Estimates that has been investigating military expenditure abroad. Speaking in a debate at the 1964 Labour Party Conference at Blackpool he said:

'Defence expenditure is bedevilling social advance all over the world and is reaching ridiculous proportions. Today our defence expenditure is running at the rate of £2,120 million per year. This great mountain of wealth is sweated out of the labour and industrial intelligence of the British people.

'It is my privilege to serve with the new Parliament as Chairman of Sub-Committee "D" of the Select Committee on Estimates which deals with military expenditure and I am appalled at the way in which the people's money is wasted—particularly was this so under the Conservative administration. There is a built-in resistance among the heads of the Defence Departments to any reduction in military expenditure.

'To give one or two examples of how the people's money is wasted, I discovered that during our last four years in Kenya, prior to independence, we spent £5½ million on permanent buildings. We built a NAAFI like a West End store and a church like a cathedral and passed the whole lot, without compensation, on to the new Government of Kenya.

'In Cyprus an underground assembly factory, air conditioned, which cost £400,000 was closed down and dismantled the week it was completed. It took eighteen months for a Cabinet decision to seep back to the builders in Cyprus who went on building, despite the decision to close this project down.

'Our defence expenditure today takes 26 per cent of all Government expenditure and 7·2 per cent each year of our total national income.

'On the so-called East of Suez Policy we spend £320 million per year without weapons on overseas bases, with weapons it costs us £500 million per year. A quarter of all military expenditure and one sixteenth of all Government expenditure.

'In the SEATO area which covers our East of Suez Policy the countries involved in the defence of this area are spending much less than ourselves. For example, Australia, one of the six richest countries in the world, spends only 4·2 per cent of her national income on defence; the Phillipines only 1·9 per cent; Japan 1·6 per cent against our 7·2 per cent and even in NATO the countries concerned, with the exception of Britain, have all been cutting back their defence expenditure.'

Mr. Edwards referred to the cost of the East of Suez Policy. How is it really possible for Parliament to assess the cost of such a policy without a searching investigation of such a policy and what it really means?

There was one sentence from a speech that Winston Churchill delivered when attacking the Labour Government in the Naval Estimates debate of 1948 that I frequently used in the Navy debates in later years.

He was attacking the Government for the large staff at the Admiralty. He said, 'What has happened has been this enormous growth of civilian officials of all kinds who have been superimposed and who make work for themselves and their descendants every day they sat in their office chairs. The whole presentation of the Admiralty staff is a scandal which any House of Commons worthy of its responsibilities should probe, scrub and cleanse.'

It got worse and not better of course when Churchill and the Tories returned to power in 1951, and worse as the years went on. But Churchill's description of the duty of the House of Commons remained.

Nobody reading the debates on the Navy Estimates of those years would realize that we had arrived in the age of nuclear warfare. Reginald Paget who for a time arrived, I do not know how, as one of the Labour Party spokesmen for the Shadow Cabinet on the Front Opposition Bench, did sometimes sound an original and critical note, especially on the occasion when he tried to find out what the role of the navy would be in the event of nuclear attack. He said that the signal that should be sent out immediately to the navy was 'Get to hell out of here'. If that was the position what exactly were we spending nearly £500 million a year on the navy for? Frequently as I asked this question I never expected an answer from the Civil Lord of the Admiralty who wound up the debate.

If there had been a Select Committee inquiry into the activities of the Admiralty in the same way as the Select Committee on Nationalized Industries inquired into the way money was spent by London Transport or the Gas Council we might have discovered the answer.

Yet I never wondered why the Admiralty came along year after year with its enormous bills. The wonder was that, seeing the ease with which it managed to get its money and the lack of serious criticism or opposition from the handful of Members who turned up, that it did not ask for more. The Admiralty officials in the box were quite justified if they regarded the House of Commons as a handful of ignoramuses who could easily be hoodwinked and bluffed because they had little real knowledge of what it was all about. When the Polaris submarine programme was superimposed upon the other Admiralty activities it got worse. A new base was announced for Faslare in the West of Scotland at an estimated cost of £20 to £25 million. By the time the Labour Government arrived in 1964 the estimated cost had risen to £45 million.

Before we were committed to the Polaris programme it should have been carefully examined by a Select Committee entrusted with the duty to 'probe, scrub and cleanse', as Churchill had urged ten years before. Of course it never was.

The Labour Government would never have needed to carry out its lengthy review of Defence Expenditure in 1965 if a Committee had been at work sifting out the information and ascertaining the facts in the previous years. In the year before the Election and during the Election spokesmen for the Labour Party repeatedly said that they would have to wait until a Labour Government was in office before it could have access to the information in order to make up its mind about policy.

What we did know was that the enormous expenditure on defence and especially that incurred overseas was one of the main causes of the financial crisis in which we found ourselves.

The case is overwhelming for a thorough re-examination of the way the House of Commons has allowed defence expenditure to lead us down the road to national bankruptcy.

In his evidence submitted to the Committee of Procedure in 1958 Sir Edmund Fellowes, the then Clerk of the House of Commons. advocated the idea of a Defence Committee.

In his memorandum he said:

'I suggest setting up a Defence Committee "to consider the Estimates of the Ministry of Defence, the three Services and the Ministry of Supply and to report what economies consistent with the policy implied in those Estimates might be effected therein and to consider such other matters as might be referred to it by the House or put before it by the Minister of Defence". I suggest that the Committee should consist of fifteen or twenty Members empowered to work through sub-committees which should be instructed to report direct to the House by the middle of May. Thus, if the Service Votes were considered in detail in Committee of Supply in June and July the Committee of Supply would have the advantage of these Reports, while some Members interested in a particular Service would have the opportunity of devoting themselves to investigating the details of it. At the same time, the Minister of Defence in his discretion could consult the Committee on any matter.'

This was another example of how the Clerks of the House are more radical and enlightened than the Government Front Bench.

Can anyone in the House of Commons really maintain that we have been adequately informed about Foreign Affairs during recent years? Prime Ministers and Foreign Ministers depart to meet their opposite numbers in other countries. When the meetings are over we get the briefest of statements and when M.P.s ask questions they are referred to these statements. Mr Harold Macmillan, when he was Prime Minister, became a master of this technique. Weeks after, the House may get its opportunity in a two-day debate. It is impossible for the Speaker to squeeze one half of those who wish to speak and to seek further information into these debates. I have been informed that in the last debate on Foreign Affairs in 1965 over eighty Members wanted to speak.

Yet this is a time when M.P.s have to make up their minds and decide on issues of vital importance to Britain and the future of the world.

Take for example the question of what is to be our future rôle in the Far East and what it is to cost us both in military expenditure and in economic consequences. Here is an issue which the House is entitled to ask a committee to examine in all its various aspects. Here both Mr Harold Wilson and Mr Enoch Powell could be called upon to explain exactly what they mean. 'East of Suez' is a phrase which might mean anything. So is the word 'commitments'. M.P.s and the country could get more real and precise information about this issue in this way, in the report of the questions and answers, than they are ever likely to get either at Question Time or indeed in a two-day Foreign Affairs debate. That not only applies to the Far East.

Mr Harold Macmillan's decision to give America a Polaris base in Scotland was, as Mr Dennis Healy said at the time, 'a matter of life and death for the British people'. But on this issue there was no adequate debate. There were secret clauses in the agreement about which we are allowed to know nothing. Mr Macmillan obliged Mr Gaitskell by not announcing the news about the Polaris agreement until, after the Labour Party Conference. Mr Macmillan did not embarrass the Leader of the Labour Party and then in turn Mr Gaitskell did not embarrass Mr Macmillan with a vote of censure. Mr Healey's initial attack was not followed up. The Polaris agreement was never submitted to the House for final approval and satisfaction.

A committee would have rendered great service to the House and the nation at the time if it could have asked Mr Macmillan to appear before it, so that he could explain and be questioned as to what it implied and what its consequences might be for us. Mr Henry Brandon's (the *Sunday Times* Washington correspondent) later revelations indicated that Mr Macmillan had his fears about what he had done himself.

History has taught us how the secret diplomacy of Sir Edward Grey led us into what we now know was one of the most ghastly futilities in the long story of the martyrdom of man—the First World War. We have apparently learned so little from this that we are content to allow our secret diplomacy to become more secret than ever.

When we nearly had the Third World War over Cuba, Britain might have been destroyed in a night without the House of Commons, which is supposed to represent the British people, having the slightest say in the matter. We would not even have been summoned to Westminster, like Parliament was in August 1914, to approve of a declaration of war! Neither would any representative body in any country in the world. Indeed the gentlemen responsible for pressing the button in Britain would never have had to account to anybody, for nobody would have survived and neither would he.

We hear a lot about the Free World, and our democracy and our Parliaments where the people's representatives decide things. In this so-called 'Free World' we can be blown into eternity the day after tomorrow without anybody consulting us about it. The Prime Minister will hardly be able to go to the House to announce after Question Time 'The House will regret to learn that I felt it my duty to press the button at midnight' because the House won't be there—and probably neither the Prime Minister unless he makes the announcement from some deep bomb-proof shelter to a nation that isn't there either.

Too much power in the making of foreign policy has become too concentrated into too few hands. If we are to survive at all we ought to do what we can to rectify this before it is too late.

CHAPTER 13

THE CRITICS OUTSIDE

When Mr Bowden, the Leader of the House, spoke at the conclusion of the debate on procedure he remarked that 'the degree of knowledge outside the House about our procedure is abysmally low'.

The only evidence he produced for this statement was that a writer in the *Observer* had referred to the green benches as red. Mr Bowden therefore came to the conclusion that he had never seen the House of Commons and so the criticisms he had made of its procedure could be dismissed.

There is always this tendency in the House of Commons to dismiss the critics as if they know nothing about it and to take up a 'Hands Off Our House' attitude. But M.P.s should be prepared to listen to the critics outside. After all it is their House too and what is happening there is surely of national concern. How are we entitled to talk so much about the need for the modernization of British industry, a theme on which there have been innumerable speeches both in the House and on the political platforms outside, if when somebody in the Press comes along with criticisms and suggestions we take the line 'What do you know about it anyhow. For God's sake shut up.'

After all, is not the House of Commons a nationalized industry and if it sets up a committee to inquire whether the efficiency of other industries is what it should be, why should it not be prepared to be inquired into too? Indeed it was an outside body, the Lawrence Committee, that inquired into the question of M.P's salaries and the House of Commons unanimously and jubilantly accepted its findings. Then has not the Post Office recently appointed an industrial consultant to inquire if any improvements are necessary in its organization?

If the House of Commons refuses to modernize itself what right has it to compulsorily modernize anything else? When it has been clearly shown that it has become a legislative bottleneck still clinging on in many ways as it did in the reign of

Queen William, have not the people outside not only the right but the duty to protest?

It certainly will be a humiliation for the House of Commons if a body of outsiders has to be called in to bring it up to date because its Members are incapable— or unwilling — of doing so.

Had the House of Commons shown itself really alive to the need for the modernisation of its procedure there would have been no need for The Study of Parliament Group to come along to its Procedure Committee with a lengthy memoranda, and for members of it to give evidence.

This body should certainly command respect. Among the supporters of the memorandum were Sir Edward Fellowes, the former Clerk of the House of Commons, and fifteen of the most eminent professors and lecturers in politics from our leading universities.

Obviously their views deserve respectful consideration. If they teach politics at the universities their views must influence thousands of students, many of whom will no doubt be in due time arriving as M.P.s.

The memorandum runs to ten pages of the Committee's Report and is an extremely useful contribution to the question of how Parliament can be modernized.

Far from being 'abysmally ignorant', the professors have obviously studied the subject in great detail and have gone to a great deal of trouble to outline constructive proposals for reform.

When Mr Herbert Bowden, the Leader of the House, gave evidence before the Select Committee of Procedure on March 26th he said:

'I still think procedure as it is will go on for another twenty years without being an embarrassment to the Government and Opposition because they are used to working it. However, it has become a botched-up sort of thing through the years simply because it has been adapted to suit the Government and Opposition of the day.'

So that in spite of all the talk about modernization the Leader of the House under a Labour Government thinks that the present state of procedure will go on for another twenty years, in spite of the criticisms that have been made of it.

Every conservative-minded traditionalist would agree with that.

Note Mr Bowden was thinking only in terms of Government and Opposition and the word Parliament never entered into it at all. Supposing any industrialist, the efficiency of whose industry had come into question, had said 'It will last another twenty years. Both sides think its okay', what would the Labour Party have said about it?

Mr Bowden was the Chief Whip of the Labour Party when it was in opposition for many years and his point of view is still the point of the Chief Whip. He is on the other side of the table, that is all, and his opposite number, the Conservative Chief Whip, would no doubt agree with him absolutely. Their function has been and, so Mr Bowden thinks, will be to shepherd their respective flocks into the division lobbies.

He turns as deaf an ear to demands for change as the head of some small family business who takes the point of view that the business has been going on these lines for the last twenty years and will continue to do so on the same lines for the next twenty.

Compare Mr Bowden's complacency with the view expressed by Professor Bernard Crick in his book *The Reform of Parliament*.

'By comparison with the popular assembly of almost any other free country Parliament has fallen hideously behind the times both in its procedures and in the facilities that it extends to its Members, and there is good ground for thinking that it would benefit from some fairly drastic internal alterations and repairs which would go far beyond mere patching. Despite the general complacency of M.P.s themselves, there has been evidence lately of public concern: flare-ups of indignation and mockery in the public Press, worried soul-searchings and reassurances in the heavier papers. Parliamentary reform has actually become a newsworthy topic. Some M.P.s are aware of a growing scepticism, even hostility, certainly bewilderment among the public; but the House as a whole seems to react only by an increasing testiness about "privilege"—such as telling journalists not to be rude to them and not to tell the public what goes on in the "private" party meetings . . . The declining effectiveness of the House has been paralleled, as we will see, by a rising efficiency of the Executive. But there is no necessary contradiction between wanting a strong Executive and wanting a more effective and efficient House of Commons. The more power we entrust to a Government to do things for us, the greater the need for it to operate amid a blaze of publicity and criticism. But there is such a contradiction at the moment because Parliament has not improved her own instruments of control, scrutiny, criticism and suggestion to keep pace with the great improvements of efficiency and increase of size in the departments of executive government. Small wonder that public comprehension of Parliament is so low that confidence is declining. Unless Parliament does something to repair its hide-bound ways this confidence may degenerate from the typical affectionate scepticism (at times so good for the pride of Ministers) into an indignant cynicism (hitherto of course a purely foreign phenomenon).

But it is not only the indignant cynicism that might endanger Parliament as an institution.

There is the indifferent cynicism which takes the form of asking 'Aren't they all the same? What's the difference between them?'

It is not only the criticism of the informed that the Labour Party should listen to but the criticism of the ignorant that does not realize the difficulties that a Labour Government has in forcing its programme through the bottleneck of the ancient parliamentary procedure. For these are the days when an enormous amount of legislation has to be passed on a great variety of matters. Even after only a year of a Labour Government it is accused of not fulfilling all the promises that were contained in a five-year programme.

In both their memorandum and in their evidence before the Select Committee the professors outlined constructive proposals for the speeding-up of legislation.

I do not see how any M.P. could object to the way they introduced their proposals. They said:

'We consider that there is a strong case for streamlining the passage of legislation, but only if the consequence is to give the House more time, facilities and procedural devices with which to obtain the information that Members require and to study, scrutinize and criticize both the workings of the whole machinery of government and the factual assumptions on which policy decisions are made.

'The greatness and the unique character of British institutions lie in the fact that it has been possible and has for long been thought desirable to have both strong Government and effective criticism of it within the House. But as the machinery of central Government is strengthened, so steps should be taken to strengthen the critical efficacy of the House of Commons and its ability to reach the public ear.

'We do not see the need for great changes in the basic character of the Procedures of Parliament. But we do see the need to make practical proposals to relate together systematically a fair number of changes of detail which have seemed for a long time, both to people inside and outside the House, no more than the commonsense of the matter of maintaining the repute and power of Parliament.

'The procedures of the House of Commons need to be modified in recognition of the fact that effective "parliamentary control" has for a long time meant not mainly the threat of overthrowing the Government in the House but also the process of influencing the Government and informing the electorate.

'So the kind of proposals we are making do not seek to change the accepted balance between the Executive and Parliament, but rather to enable Parliament to perform its traditional role more efficiently and effectively.'

They outlined their constructive and practical proposals on the presentation of bills to Parliament, on the simplifying of bills, on Second Reading and Committee procedure, on Delegated Legislation, on Financial Resolutions, on Lords Amendments and on Finance and Private Members' Bills. One would have thought that the Leader of the House and a Government anxious to get its legislation through would have welcomed them. They certainly impressed the Select Committee.

But instead of that the Leader of the House regarded them with suspicion and hostility and an attitude which seemed like saying 'Mind your own business. Keep off the grass.' In this he was of course doing just what R. A. Butler had done before him when the Select Committee on Procedure had been asked to recommend some parliamentary reforms in 1959.

Of course they were in one respect daring. They actually suggested that some M.P.s should do more work in the mornings.

In their recommendations on morning sittings and other arrangements for debates they said:

'We draw attention to the fact that extra time would be available for debate by the House as a whole as a result of our proposals for Public Legislation for the removal of the committee and report stage of bills from the floor of the House and for delegated legislation.

'We recommend that more use be made of the mornings for the work of the House but only for, in addition to committee work as at present (which would in any case be expanded under our proposals):

'Ad hoc committees to debate non-controversial motions or matters of interest to limited numbers of Members (for example, the problems of particular industries or regions). The procedure would be the same as that employed by the Scottish Grand Committee in debating Scottish matters referred to them.

'Debates on the Reports of Royal Commissions, of other important inquiries and of select committees.

'If it is suggested that sufficient time or Members would not be available for the extra work that would follow from our proposals for the increased work of committees, we point out that:

'It is reasonable to suppose following the Lawrence Report that more Members will be available for the service of the House in the mornings.'

One of the reasons that the Lawrence Committee recommended an increase in Members' salaries was that a large number would be available for committee work in the mornings.

Were then the professors' proposals so unreasonable?

Mr Enoch Powell had objected to having more Members on the Estimates Committee because 'it is a very heavy burden on the shoulders of it if it is properly done and I feel there is a limit to the number of Members who are available to do that work at the required standard'.

This point was put to Professor Wiseman, of Exeter University, by Mr Carol Johnson during his examination.

'Under your scheme there is to be a substantial number of these specialist committees with a membership of, I think you suggested, between fifteen and twenty. That is going to occupy the attention of a considerable proportion of the House. When do you visualize they should most conveniently meet without putting too great a burden on Members?'

Professor Wiseman replied:

'We had thought this would occupy something between 120 and 140 Members of the House when there was a fully fledged system of select committees covering the whole field of administration. Now, so far as when they meet is concerned, we have assumed that normally they would meet in the afternoons, which I understand happens now. I realize this would be on a much larger scale than at present exists. One would hope, incidentally, that there would not be too many division bells to interrupt their continuity of deliberation. As to whether or not it would ever be possible for them to meet in the mornings, I think we all felt in a way that involves such a decision of high policy about the whole organisation of the work of the House of Commons that we did not dare to put forward a recommendation on it. The other thing, if I may, Sir, just throw it out, is that it is the view of some of us academics that it is a pity that, so far, no use whatever has ever been made of Standing Order No. 10 which permits the adjournment of the House in order to enable committees to meet. Some of us feel, rightly or wrongly, that perhaps even one afternoon a week or one afternoon a fortnight, as the case may be, could more profitably be spent in this kind of committee work than in some of the things that occupy the time of the House as a whole. You will forgive me; this is just sticking my neck out.'

Why should it be considered unreasonable for between 120 and 140 M.P.s to be asked to serve on specialist committees?

After all there are 630 M.P.s in the House of Commons and the electors sent them there because they thought they were capable of representing them.

Mr Enoch Powell obviously takes the view that less than a quarter of M.P.s are capable or willing to do their job.

In their evidence the professors give the reasons why specialist committees would improve the efficiency of the House of Commons.

'Specialist Committees are needed to scrutinize the actions of government in their own fields, to collect, discuss, and report evidence relevant to proceedings in Parliament, whether legislative or other. The main weakness in Parliament's present methods of scrutinizing administration, and indeed of debating policy matters, is the limited ability to obtain the background facts and understanding essential for any detailed criticism of administration or any informed discussion of policy. Specialist committees, working on lines similar to those of the Estimates Committee or Nationalized Industries Committee (itself a fairly recently established specialist committee), could go a long way to remedy this. They would be mainly concerned with administration and would normally seek to avoid matters of policy which are controversial between the major political parties. They could carry out valuable inquiries into matters of direct concern to many ordinary citizens, such as hospital administration, prison rules, training of teachers and agricultural research. Their reports would be fully argued and their evidence would be detailed, but we do not envisage that the deliberations of such committees would be reported or that they should debate publicly.'

If the figures given by the professors are correct, and they were not challenged, then 120 M.P.s would serve on specialist committees considering the activities of different Government departments and would have the satisfaction that they were dealing directly with the affairs of the nation, and their reports would contain valuable and useful information for other M.P.s.

One of the objections by the Leader of the House was that it would mean that civil servants could be questioned by a committee of Members. He said:

'I should think it quite wrong for a civil servant to attend a Sub-Committee of the Estimates Committee or a similar committee and be cross-questioned by that Committee on the work of the department in which he is employed, if in fact these questions concerned policy.'

M.P.s who have served on town councils or county councils will find difficulty in understanding why civil servants in Government Departments should be regarded as untouchables whereas at the committees of local authorities their officials are present at the committee meetings to give information and advice. The business of local authorities could not be carried out under any other conditions. A Medical Officer of Health for a county council is regularly present at the Public Health Committee to give information and answer questions. Why, if a specialist committee were to be set up to inquire into Ministry of Health problems should not the Chief Medical Officers under the Ministry not be asked to do the same thing. Both are public servants. In the last result of course the county council Medical Officer of Health would not be responsible for decisions of policy, it would be the Public Health Committee and finally the County Council. Under a specialist committee the Minister of Health would still have the responsibility for answering questions on policy in the House of Commons.

In the House of Commons the words 'ministerial responsibility' are used like one uses the words 'Holy Ghost'.

Of course there is ministerial responsibility but the idea that Ministers are the only persons responsible for policy is quite a wrong one. Members of Parliament are responsible too and they have a right to judge policy in the light of the best possible information available.

Why should there be this objection to M.P.s meeting civil servants as councillors meet their officials? It would certainly lead to M.P.s knowing what is going on in government and a greater realization of their responsibility for it.

What would one think of a town councillor or a county councillor who refused to take part on any of the committees or was refused the opportunity of doing so if he wished to do so? All councillors of course do not serve on all committees, they specialize, and one fails to see the objection why M.P.s should not do so also.

The *Observer* article about which Mr Bowden was so contemptuous appeared under the headline 'A Waste of Good M.P.s'. From my experience of the Parliament elected in October 1964 I would be inclined to make it read 'A Waste of Good Young M.P.s'.

A new M.P. arrives at the House of Commons full of enthusiasm for his job. He gets the opportunity of making his first maiden speech and after that has to wait his turn to be called, often waiting many weary hours unsuccessfully trying to catch the Speaker's eye. If he is not pushful or not too good a speaker the House frightens him and he ceases to regularly attend the debates and hangs about in the smoke room or the tea room or the bar waiting for the division bell or not coming to the House at all except when there is a three-line or an urgent two-line whip.

That is the story of too many M.P.s whose Parliamentary duties would interest them and whose services would be utilized if they had the opportunity of serving on committees where their knowledge and experience would be useful.

It is a complete mistake to think that the debaters and orators and those who succeed in getting into the parliamentary limelight are the only good M.P.s or good local authority members.

Some of the best councillors that I have worked with on local authorities have been men and women who do not shine as speakers on public platforms. Their gifts and abilities lie in different directions. One of the ablest local authority members I have met in my lifetime was a man who always spoke in short staccato sentences and never made a lengthy speech. But when he intervened in any discussion he had always some relevant point to make and he always had something very pertinent to say. I have seen that over and over again in the House of Commons too. These are the men and women whose services and sense of public duty the community and Parliament needs as much as the orators and the spell-binders.

Are the professors and lecturers in politics at the universities the only ones who realize what is wrong in Parliament and want to see it changed?

But it is not only in the more political weeklies and dailies that the question 'Is Parliament Out of Date?' is being asked.

In November 1965 *The Sun* published three articles on the subject. In its first it said:

'Somewhere along the line something has gone wrong with Parliament. A sense of frustration has settled on the back benches of the Commons. Many M.P.s believe that they have become voting machines whose ideas and plans are neither sought nor listened to.

'Above all they believe that there are barriers which prevent them working as they believe elected representatives should.

'This frustration is felt on both sides of the House, but it is the Labour back-benchers who are the more bitter and disillusioned.

'The feeling has become more marked since the Commons debated reform on October 27th and heard the Government shatter widespread hopes for changes.

'Front-bench Conservatives also firmly hold the view that the old hands know best.

'Sir Martin Redmayne, Shadow Minister of Transport, seemed to be speaking for the Government as well as the Opposition when he said in the reform debate:

' "I hold strongly that we should not act hastily in favour of reform simply because Members find circumstances of Parliament wearisome or irritating.

' "They should not dismiss too lightly the wisdom of their colleagues."

'Parliament is still hidebound to the medieval tradition of government where gentlemen from the shires and boroughs made the long and difficult journey to Westminster only if their constituents had a grievance to be raised.'

The Sun investigator, Mr Malcolm Stuart, put in more popular language for the man in the street what the professors had said in their memorandum.

The Sun investigator interviewed several M.P.s who gave their views on the proposed setting up of specialist committees.

Among them was Mr Jo Grimond, the Leader of the Liberal Party, who said:

'To be able to question civil servants would be a parliamentary power for M.P.s. It would have to be circumscribed and not abused. We must be realists however and admit that a Minister cannot be responsible for everything that goes on in his department. His advisers should no longer remain anonymous in the background. Standing committees of between twenty and thirty Members should meet regularly, get at what is happening and bring the influence of informed discussion to bear on the subject.'

On the question of reforming Parliament Mr Grimond, the Liberal, is less Conservative than the Labour Leader of the House. He too sees the importance of M.P.s being able to question civil servants. One can agree with him that this power should not be abused and that the Minister who takes the responsibility in Parliament is the one who has made the decision which he must defend as long as the ministerial system continues. But Mr Grimond has grasped the point that the special information and experience that the Civil Service has acquired should be more open to M.P.s. No local authority would dream of passing estimates for a housing scheme or a school or a police station or a public swimming bath without discussing with its officials their estimates of its costs. Then why should not a committee of M.P.s be able to question officials more fully about the estimated costs of any enterprise that Parliament is asked to approve. If there had been a Foreign Office Committee going carefully into what was involved in the Suez Expedition we would have been saved a substantial amount of public money. Dickens has satirized the government official who complained about a persistent inquirer because 'he wanted to know, you know'. M.P.s are entitled to know and get the fullest possible information about public expenditure. They are not of course entitled to be pilloried for a ministerial decision with which they might or might not agree. But there is now too much of a barrier between the civil servant and the M.P.

Mr John Mendelson, Labour M.P. for Penistone, was not, however, enthusiastic about specialist committees. He expressed the point of view that 'Ministers would be able to manipulate the committees by taking Members into their confidence and then forbidding them to reveal matters discussed on security grounds'. 'I cannot believe that civil servants would really tell a committee any more than their Ministers instructed them.'

Now it is quite possible that some information that a Member might ask for, say in a Defence Committee, might be withheld from an official report on security grounds. That is the practice today. But refusing to inform M.P.s empowered by the House of Commons to call for persons and papers is a different matter. Nobody, for example, has asked for a Select Committee to inquire into the expenditure and activities of the Secret Service, although its expenditure, incidentally, has greatly increased during recent years. The Official Secrets Act can be enforced against M.P.s as well as anybody else. As long as the Arms Race and the Cold War goes on every country engaged in it will continue to employ spies and prostitutes and homosexuals and other shady characters to get secret information from the enemy. Indeed if a Select Committee on the Secret Service were possible, the evidence and information and the examination of witnesses would be the sensational best seller of all time. But nobody has suggested that. Mr Khrushchev came the nearest when he suggested ironically that it would be cheaper for the Big Powers to exchange their secret information.

One often wonders, however, when one receives the answer that 'it is not in the public interest to give the information', whether this is not so much because it is feared that the potential enemy may get the information (the odds are that he has already got it) but that the information had better be hidden from the British taxpayer.

However only a fraction of public expenditure that needs inquiry into could come under the security objection and any Minister who told a civil servant to withhold information from a committee of M.P.s because he wanted it hushed up should be exposed and dismissed. Ministers are the servants of Parliament, not dictators.

Of course there is always the possibility of a Minister hoodwinking a committee and there is also the possibility of a committee being packed with stooges and 'yes' men. But it only needs one, two or three Members to be persistent and determined to bring some matter to light which the Minister might prefer to remain hidden but which it is in the public interest that Parliament should know.

Mr Mendelson thought M.P.s would be better served by private enterprise. He said:

'I want an office and private secretary for each Member, a graduate research officer for every four Members, a greatly enlarged library with specialist staff; free travel in this country to see what industry and Government departments are doing; subscriptions to many national and international journals and increased facilities to travel abroad. All this will provide a conscientious M.P. with the information that committees will only grope at. I want full facilities to find out myself.'

Mr Mendelson's idea that in addition to all the other facilities an M.P. should have one-fourth of a private detective to himself is a novel one, but what would the Minister do when the private detectives came along? Would he give them a special press conference or would he not hoodwink them too. I am not against keeping Mr Mendelson's 100 private detectives in reserve but I think the specialist committees should be allowed to try first.

The Sun investigator inquired what happened in other countries where the committee system works. This was especially interesting because Lord Butler when he was at the dispatch box dismissed the whole idea of special committees on the grounds that Britain did not want committees 'à l'Americaine', a fine mouthful of Anglo-Saxon prejudice and ignorance calculated to appeal to those who think British institutions and habits are the best in the world because they happened accidentally to be born here. The wonder is that he did not add that the members of the committee would be forced to give up good old British beef and tea and dine on frogs boiled in Coco Cola as well. *The Sun* man said of America, 'Committees of the United States Congress have sometimes abused their power — the late Senator McCarthy's private Star Chamber, for example.

'But in the opinion of American experts on government this does not invalidate the exercise of the power.'

Herr Werner Blischke, head of the legal department of the Bundestag, said:

'The committees themselves consist almost entirely of experts—lawyers on the legal committees, former civil servants on the civil service committee, farmers forming "a green front" on the agricultural committee. The trouble is that they are all so qualified that when they speak in the House they tend to baffle the non-experts into silence.'

Which is exactly what happens in the House of Commons

now when legal matters and agricultural matters are being discussed. That always happens anyway. But the conclusion was, 'Despite this the committees are thus able to deal in detail with specific legislation and polish it up. Our bills, as a result, are more precise than yours.'

But nobody is suggesting that we should take over the legislative habits of stupid or ignorant foreigners and implant their constitutions on ours. There is nothing inherently foreign in committees. They would only be a development of what we already have here.

The Sun investigator concluded his series of articles by saying:

'That so many Members are dissatisfied and frustrated by the traditions and limitations of Parliament must indicate that something is wrong.

'In fact, the Commons have got themselves so tied up with tradition that many Members believe effective government is being hampered.

'The older Members know how to turn tradition and procedure to their own advantage. The younger M.P.s do not. They ask why they should be stifled because they do not know as much about the rules of Parliament.

'The writing on the wall is plain to see. Unless the Commons are prepared to put their House in order, it is unlikely that they will attract men and women of the calibre needed to govern Britain in the last third of the twentieth century. Frustration is not a good basis for sound government.'

Mr Bowden countered this last remark that if he were to retire tomorrow there would be no lack of candidates for his seat. There is no doubt about that, but that is no argument for taking the line that nothing is going to be done to change parliamentary procedure for the next twenty years.

CHAPTER 14

THE SCOTTISH PENITENTIARY

Whenever a Conservative M.P. came in to take his seat during the last months of the Conservative Government the cry went up from the Labour benches below the gangway, 'Scottish Grand Committee for you'. His vote at the by-election had gone down and his drafting to the Scottish Grand Committee was the penalty. When a new Tory face appeared there one wondered what he had done to incur the displeasure of his Whips.

The reason of course was that the Tories did not have a majority on the Scottish Grand Committee and so it was necessary to add English M.P.s who had no interest at all in Scottish business and if they could not get pairs (not so easy in those days when Scots Labour M.P.s were anxious to defeat the Government) they either had to sit listening to lengthy Scottish speeches on subjects about which they knew nothing or hang about in the corridors in case the division bell rang. If you ask old hands whether they have served on the Scottish Grand Committee the usual answer is 'Yes. Never again.'

In the Parliament that was elected in 1964, although the Labour majority in Scotland was substantially increased, the Labour Government had only the narrowest majority on the Committee. Because the membership of the Committee must reflect the composition of the House more English M.P.s had to be added, reinforced by an Ulster Unionist, whose crime I have never discovered!

This is why any proposal suggesting Home Rule for Scotland can usually get a sympathetic cheer from the Conservative benches.

As long as the Labour Party has only a small majority in the House there will be no great enthusiasm for any changes which would mean the Scots retreating to Scotland and the Welsh returning to Wales, for that would leave the English Tories in control at Westminster. If the Scots were to demand representation on the Scottish Grand Commitee according to their numerical strength, Mr Iain Macleod has been quick to remind us the English would demand an English majority on committees dealing with purely English bills and in these the Labour Government would always be in the minority.

But there is obviously something wrong when M.P.s have to spend their mornings listening to speeches about something they know nothing about and care less.

This problem will continue until Labour is in control of Westminster with a majority of Labour M.P.s in England as well as in Scotland or Wales, as was the case in the big changeover in 1945.

When that comes, and I hope it will come soon, some changes in the way Scotland and Wales are governed will be necessary.

One of the points made in the memorandum by the Study of Parliament Group was that Scottish and Welsh questions should be asked and answered at the Scottish and Welsh Committees.

This is a reform which I have suggested for many years although, I must say, with little support from my Scots Labour colleagues. Their case is that Scotland must not be driven off the floor of the House and that Scottish interests would suffer if this were done. I have never been able to understand this objection, for the Scottish Committee Room has a floor too. It would give Scots an hour to raise questions with Scots Ministers, say an hour once a fortnight, whereas under present arrangements they may get that once a month.

There would not be so much reason to rush through questions and there would be opportunity for more supplementaries. There would be just the same publicity in the Scottish press and the wireless, for the journalists would have more time to get their reporting done for the evening press and radio and indeed might get on to the one o'clock news too.

Why then should Scots insist on taking up the time of the House and indeed have less time to put questions to other Ministers themselves? Another suggestion that has been made is that the Scots could have their questions at times when English Ministers are answering purely English questions — e.g. the Minister for Education, the Minister for Housing and Local Government and the Minister of Health.

Why should there be this fascination for the floor of the House and performing at the dispatch box when there is such a good case for ending the congestion at Question Time and indeed getting better opportunities upstairs?

The Welsh Committee is only a recent institution and the Secretary for Wales has only a fraction of the powers of the Secretary for Scotland, but I think that the Welsh questions might also go upstairs although up to the present the Welsh show no signs of filling up the Order Paper with their questions and have not so much reason to be so inquisitive as the Scots.

Not only could the Secretary for Scotland answer questions at the Scottish Grand Committee but other Ministers such as the Minister of Labour, the Minister of Power and the President of the Board of Trade whose activities the Scots M.P.s are also greatly concerned with at a time when Scotland is calling for more industries.

Why then should this proposal not be given a fair trial? If it failed we could always go back to the old procedure, although perhaps the English M.P.s, once they had got rid of us, might not be enthusiastic to welcome us back. But my contention is that it would be good for Scotland and good for the House.

Then what about Scottish business, cannot something be done about that? Could not more use be made of the Scottish Grand Committee? The custom in the past has been to give Scotland whole days in the House to discuss Scottish issues while the English M.P.s take a day off to go to the Royal garden parties or to the Derby or Ascot and other occasions like that. Then Scotland has the floor of the House and is welcome to it, and there are vast empty spaces on the benches as the small number of Scots battle it out.

There are of course the days when the Scottish Estimates are taken upstairs. This is a comparatively recent innovation, better than nothing, but no vote is taken and as the sitting only lasts from 10.30 to 1.0, two and a half hours, in which a good deal of time is taken up by the official spokesman of the Government and the Opposition and so there is not much chance for back benchers on either side.

Why should there not be Select Committees for Scotland on the lines that have been already suggested for other Government departments?

Has not the time come for an advance in introducing a larger measure of democratic government for Scottish affairs?

I

In the Cabinet Scotland is represented by the Secretary of State for Scotland and he is the supreme political overlord north of the Border.

In the Parliament elected in 1964 there is a Minister of State for Scotland, an Under Secretary in the House of Lords and two Under Secretaries in the House of Commons. Scotland has thus a small inner government of its own with its own Ministers for Agriculture, Education, Housing, Local Government, etc.

The Secretary for Scotland keeps on having more duties placed on his shoulder. In his day Mr Tom Johnston used to say that he was the General Pooh Bah of Scotland.

A conscientious, hard-working Secretary for Scotland under the present system is bound to be overworked and with every additional piece of legislation the burdens on his shoulders weigh him down and this has been very noticeable since the war. The variety of administrative problems that he has to deal with has considerably increased.

Why should not the committee system be tried in Scotland both to ease the burdens on the Secretary for Scotland and the other Ministers and to give Scottish M.P.s a greater responsibility for Scottish government? I see no reason at all why there should not be set up Scottish committees for, say, Education, Agriculture, Housing, Health and Local Government. These committees would in effect be sub-committees of the Scottish Grand Committee and consist of between fifteen and twenty members reporting their activities to the Scottish Grand Committee, as a sub-committee of a county council reports to the county council.

There are seventy-one Members from Scotland, and there is no reason why M.P.s who are anxious to do so should not be on more than one committee.

Nobody can be satisfied with the way things are run now. At the one end is the overworked and harassed Secretary for Scotland and on the other hand M.P.s with considerable experience of Scottish Affairs which is not utilised.

Take for example the case of Scottish agriculture. Scotland has a separate Scottish Department for Agriculture but Scottish M.P.s have very few opportunities of discussing in the detail that is required Agricultural Estimates, policy and the problems that have to be faced at a time when agriculture is going through so many fundamental changes. At the last meeting of the Scottish Committee on Estimates when agriculture came up for consideration the spokesman for the Opposition complained that the subject had not been discussed for three years because when Labour was in Opposition it had not been chosen because the majority of Labour M.P.s were from industrial constituencies.

This Conservative M.P. definitely had a point. Over and over again on the rare occasions when the Committee discussed agriculture one had the spectacle of Sir David Robertson, the Member for Caithness and Sutherland, protesting that although he represented a large Highland constituency he had not had the opportunity of speaking because the short debate had to finish at one o'clock.

A Scottish Agricultural Committee could, I believe, do extremely useful work for agriculture in Scotland. The M.P.s for Highland constituencies would not then feel frustrated and questions could be then seriously discussed which are only hinted at now. There is a good deal of specialist experience that could be called on, there are M.P.s with considerable knowledge of farming and others—for example, Sir Alec Douglas Home— with a lifetime experience of fishing and sporting life. I have listened many times to Sir Alec in the House of Commons, but too little on the subject he knows most about. He could do far more useful work sitting round the table in a Scottish Agricultural Committee than he was ever able to do in 10 Downing Street. This is not just an excursion into controversial political problems but the plain truth, and Sir Alec knows it as well as I do.

Then there is Scottish education, which is vitally important for the whole future of Scotland. Would it not gain if there were a Scottish Education Committee meeting say once a month getting to grips with problems that urgently need to be found and which are either dealt with superficially or almost completely in the hands of officialdom in Edinburgh? On both sides of the House there are university graduates who have spent years in the schools and men and women who have been members of education committees with years of experience of the practical administrative problems of education. Why cannot all this knowledge and experience be utilized? Everybody interested in education knows that far more thought and drive should be devoted to it than is possible under the present system.

Housing and local government is a sphere that there is no doubt a committee could do useful work.

On the Labour benches there are ex-city, county and town councillors who have lived with the question of housing for years and know it from A to Z. Glasgow Members include an ex-Lord Provost and ex-conveners and members of Glasgow Corporation Housing Committee whose practical experience and knowledge is now largely wasted because of the present set-up in national government.

Under our present Parliamentary arrangement Scots M.P.s travel down on Monday by plane or train and return on Thursday nights or Fridays knowing that they have done an enormous amount of time hanging about when they could have been spending their time on work which would really have interested them and in which they could have made useful contributions. These committees should have the power to meet in Edinburgh and Glasgow. Many days in the session could be utilized in this way when Parliament is discussing non-controversial or purely English legislation. It need make no difference to the voting at Westminster for pairing could operate with Members of both parties being engaged on Parliamentary work elsewhere and proxy voting should be arranged.

With such a change in procedure Scotland would have more attention devoted to its government and its problems than it has ever had before.

The case for Wales is rather different although the general argument holds good. Wales has not its own system of law and local government but it has its own special problems which would receive greater attention than they do today.

Indeed the question might well be considered whether some regional political devolution is not due. For planning and industrial purposes the country is already divided into areas. There is the North East Area and the South East Area with their own special problems.

I do not of course suggest that all these changes in government could be effected overnight. There is always violent and stubborn resistance to change from well-established institutions and those who think that if we decide to do something that was not done the day before yesterday, that we are plunging into the unknown.

Dr Horace King gave it as his opinion that it took ten years for a new idea about Parliament to be accepted. Sidney Webb put it at twenty and others more than that. But if we really mean it when we talk about modernization we had better begin.

We have got to get out of our heads the idea that this wonderful Westminster, the mother of Parliaments, with its glorious traditions and all the rest of it is so perfect that it must go on unaltered or slowly from precedent to precedent without any need for necessary change.

CHAPTER 15

'RAZE IT TO THE GROUND'

What about the Palace of Westminster where Parliament meets and where M.P.s have to work? Does that not need to be modernized? There are of course those who think that it should be left alone and not interfered with. But in recent years there has been a steady demand that the whole place needs to be thoroughly overhauled to make it less of a museum and more of a workshop.

During the proceedings of the Select Committee that inquired into the future of the administration of the Palace of Westminster a Conservative M.P., Sir Harmar Nicholls, said 'Any self-respecting efficiency expert would say "Raze the building to the ground and build a new one" '. I would hesitate to do this—at least not yet.

One of the younger M.P.s, Mr Tam Dalzell, who represents Mid Lothian, recently took the trouble to make an extensive survey and examination of the huge building to see how it is being used and how it could be adapted for the needs of today.

He published an interesting account of his investigations in an article in *The Architects' Journal* for August 19, 1964. He wrote:

'One of my troubles is that fact-finding is quite incredibly difficult. When I wrote to the Law Lords (Lords Reid, Radcliffe, Evershed, Morris of Borth-y-Gest, Hodson, Guest, Pearce, Upjohn, Donovan), asking them with all the courtesy at my command how many days per year and how many hours per day they used their ground floor individual offices just by the strangers' dining-room, all I got was a series of nifty letters, telling me to ask the Lord Great Chamberlain. Be correct, and be taken round by the Lord Chamberlain's secretary, as I was when I first knew the date of the accommodation debate, and find that "the Lord Great Chamberlain has given me instructions that you are only to be shown the public accommodation"—which is a fat lot of use if one is serious about finding the truth about what goes on in the 1,500 rooms in the Palace of Westminster.

'The real trouble with the Lord Great Chamberlain's secretary's tour was his ignorance, as a guide, of what accommodation actually existed (unless one credits him with being less than frank, which would go ill with one so intimately connected with the trappings of chivalry). Therefore I undertook a series of private fact-finding expeditions, which have been the source of a host of complaints by the Lord Great Chamberlain and the Chairman of Committees in writing to the Labour Chief Whip and Leader, and to the Speaker, but not directly to me . . .

'To start with, I reproduce the electoral roll of the Palace of Westminster, showing those who have residences. In spite of the best efforts of the Stokes Committee, some of whose members are under the delusion that they reduced the number of residents in the palace, the population has grown.

Census 1921 ... 17 usually resident
Census 1951 ... 19 usually resident
Census 1961 ... 25 usually resident'

Mr Dalzell cast envious eyes on the rooms occupied by the Lord Chancellor.

'The Lord Chancellor has twenty-nine private rooms, most, if not all of which could be converted with minimum delay into M.P.s' offices. In addition his office, brought to the palace in emergency conditions by Lord Jowett, has twenty-four rooms.

'The secretaries to Sir George Coldstream, secretary to the Lord Chancellor, have superbly elegant accommodation—not for them the frowns of the inspectors of the Offices and Shops Act, who would have a fit if they visited some of the rooms upstairs where M.P.s work together among single filing cabinets. . . .'

Then there was the accommodation of the Sergeant at Arms.

'On one matter the Lord Great Chamberlain's secretary was quite right. "There's a great deal of fat in the Commons accommodation." If we follow Miss Jennie Lee, and "put a circle round the Chamber, and make certain that we examine every inch of that area to consider how it is being used" we should come to the mansion of the Sergeant at Arms, which has between twelve and seventeen rooms. Perhaps I am not duly reverential towards the findings of the Stokes or Stanhope committees, but I cannot think how they let themselves be persuaded of the necessity that the deputy Sergeant at Arms should occupy four strategically placed rooms, plus more space. If the Government Chief Whip can motor home each night, I'm certain that the sergeants could give up their residences near the hub of Parliament and transfer to St James's Palace.'

Mr Dalzell then turned his attention to Mr Speaker.

'I would cast covetous eyes on the Speaker's house, said by the

Observer to have sixty rooms. With all the respect that I can muster, I feel that the Speaker, by an act of generosity, might return his library, originally planned by the architect for the use of the House of Commons but commandeered by Mr Speaker Dennison for the use of his family, to the Commons for whom it was originally intended. . . .

'The first prerequisite for rationalization of existing space is that the House of Commons should be its own master. With this in view, I organized the following early day motion, which within twenty-four hours won the support of eighty of my most respected colleagues: "That an humble address be presented to Her Majesty praying that the control of the Royal Palace of Westminster be transferred to a House of Commons Commission, under the chairmanship of Mr Speaker; and to amend the powers of the Lord Great Chamberlain accordingly."

'But it is not only for reasons of principle that I believe the Lord Great Chamberlain must cease to have anything to do with the Palace of Westminster. Successive Lord Great Chamberlains have fallen down badly on the job. Their job should have been to exploit every nook and corner of the building to its optimum use. The charge I make against the Lord Great Chamberlains is that they have not stirred themselves to attempt a rationalization of space. Any concern they have shown seems to have been biased towards aesthetic considerations.

'The 140 rooms which I reckon could be taken over for the immediate use of Members of the Commons (and this figure excludes peers' individual rooms, and for example the five smoking rooms allotted to Opposition peers) are few compared to what *could* be converted into offices.'

New brooms are certainly apt to sweep clean and Mr Dalzell definitely took on a big job when he started his campaign for the eviction of the Lord Chamberlain, the Sergeant at Arms and the hierarchy of the lawyers from the Palace of Westminster. No one anticipates that they will acquiesce in their eviction to St James's Palace, the Temple and the other places suggested by a young M.P. in a hurry. But Mr Dalzell did succeed in throwing a new light on some of the darker places in the palace and marked another advance in the campaign that had been carried on for years by Mr Charles Pannell, who when the Wilson Government was formed found himself Minister of Works in the excellent strategic position for getting something done to bring much needed changes at Westminster, and to make the House of Commons the real master in its own House.

On April 26, 1965, it was announced that Her Majesty the

Queen had generously agreed that the control, use and occupation of the Palace of Westminster should pass from her control to the control of the two Houses of Parliament. Previous to that supreme control was vested in the Lord Great Chamberlain. When the House of Commons was sitting, control was delegated on his behalf to the Sergeant at Arms, acting on behalf of Mr Speaker. The Select Committee on Procedure that later examined the problem of Westminster was informed by the Sergeant at Arms that 'at week-ends and during recesses control reverted to the Lord Great Chamberlain' and 'he agreed that at such times the system was "messy" '.

Under a new system of control announced by the Prime Minister control of that part of the Palace of Westminster and the precincts now occupied by or on behalf of the House of Commons is vested in Mr Speaker on behalf of the House of Commons at all times, whether the House is sitting or not.

The Select Committee which was set up to recommend means to assist in these new duties imposed on him took evidence from the Clerk of the House, the Sergeant at Arms, the Sergeant at Arms of the House of Lords, and the Minister of Works. It recommended that a Sessional Committee of the House to be called the House of Commons Sessional Committee should be set up to advise Mr Speaker on the control of the accommodation and control and services in that part of the Palace of Westminster and its precincts ocupied by or on behalf of the House of Commons.

This in itself constituted a major change in the way things had been run in the House of Commons for centuries.

People outside will naturally ask 'Why wasn't this done long ago?' The sign DEAD SLOW is one of the signs that motorists see when they drive into the precincts at Westminster. To clear up misunderstandings I always explain to visitors that this is only a sign for motorists and not the ancient motto of the place.

Visitors to the Terrace of the House of Commons, especially foreign visitors, often bring cameras with them expecting to take photographs, only to be stopped just at the right moment when they are focused for a splendid photograph of the Terrace and Westminster bridge and the river, by a policeman who warns them that photographs are not allowed except by special permit.

A question was put to the Sergeant at Arms of the House of Lords, who has been in charge of security arrangements, as to why this was necessary.

Mr Bowden asked him:

'It has been suggested to me that it was made for the protection of Members of the House of Commons and the House of Lords. A Member might be photographed with half a pint of beer in his hand and his constituents might not like it. Was this one of the reasons?'

'Yes. A picture was taken some years ago of the Lord Chancellor of the day upsetting a glass of sherry. It was very undignified and unfortunate. It was that kind of picture which was thought undesirable.'

Which to many people will not seem a very sensible reason why there should be this security ban for harmless photographs being taken on the Terrace. The M.P. with his half pint and the Lord Chancellor with his sherry can surely take some risks!

It is hoped that the changeover in control will result in greater accommodation being available for Members, including those who wish to have rooms of their own.

But the new arrangements do not alter the position that a very large part of the Palace of Westminster is still held by the House of Lords, whose members have not the constituency duties of M.P.s. Only a very small minority of peers attend the House of Lords at all regularly and there is really no justifiable reason for them holding on to so many rooms.

Mr Pannell was asked a question by Sir Herbert Butcher on this point.

'Would the Minister confirm that as a result of handing over this portion of the Palace of Westminster for the use of the Commons every opportunity for securing additional accommodation now used by the Lords or by the officers of the Lords has completely disappeared?'

Ruefully Mr Pannell had to admit that this was so.

Sir Herbert Butcher: We are now confined in a marked area for an indefinite future period and can never get any more out of them?

The Chairman: Until such time as Her Majesty gives another instruction?

Mr Pannell: I do not think there is any doubt about that. Although I was fascinated by the Lords side of the palace a good many years ago I have thought for a long time now we should better our own conditions by providing new accommodation for ourselves rather than by having new accommodation at that end of the palace. But the answer to your question is undoubtedly, yes.

So at the one end of the Palace, across the frontier where the carpet becomes red instead of green, there will continue to be hundreds of rooms rarely used, indeed hardly used at all, while on the other side of the frontier the authorities have a perpetual headache in trying to find a few square feet for the people who want a little room in which to work.

So the struggle between the haves and the have-nots goes on in the Palace of Westminster itself.

Unless of course somebody suggests to Her Majesty that she should give another instruction just to save her subjects having to pay big bills for alterations to the premises which would not be necessary if their Lordships were relieved of their unused floor space.

Of course there was a lot in the remark of Sir Harmar Nicholls, 'Any self-respecting efficiency expert would say "Raze this building to the ground and build a new one"'. Indeed it was perhaps the most sensible thing said in the whole proceedings. An efficiency expert who studies time and motion in our big factories would probably come to the conclusion that a Member of the House of Commons was wasting sixty per cent of his time and a member of the House of Lords ninety-nine per cent of it.

We owe the continued existence of the House of Commons as it is to the influence of Winston Churchill who after the Chamber had been burnt out by one of Hitler's bombs wanted the old place all rebuilt as it was before. That is why there is no seat for every Member and why when the House is crowded out for a big debate so many Members have to stand at the bar, sit up in the gallery or sit on the steps on the gangways. Churchill, of course, had been a long time in the place and there he had fought his battles and made his great historic speeches. Every cock is said to prefer its own particular dung-hill, and one can understand the old man's point of view. But was there really the need to humour him to that extent? Yet having done it is there any need to take it for granted that it will be there for a thousand years? Sir Harmar Nicholls certainly had a point but it is too early to consider razing it to the ground, not too late.

We had better wait for a decade or so to see whether a megaton bomb does the job for us, for with the West and the East piling up the missiles, the rockets and the bombs the Russians, or the Chinese, might succeed in doing what Hitler did not succeed in doing. The Palace of Westminster and the Kremlin might well be razed to the ground overnight, to the great delight of the surviving architects if there are any.

If we had not been in such a hurry after the war, we were comfortably established in the House of Lords anyway and there was much more need to rebuild London and house its homeless than to be in such a hurry in building the debating chamber of the Commons as it had been in the time of Gladstone and Disraeli.

Had we done that we could have had something like the big Shell building that now dominates the skyline on the south side of the Thames, where there would have been modern lighting and ventilation and heating and convenience for everybody, a building that nobody need be ashamed of. It would at least have shown that Parliament realized the need for the modernization of Britain in the electronic age.

Now that we are to have great new buildings in the area of Whitehall the Palace of Westminster will tend to look more and more like an ancient museum. There is definitely a case for keeping it as a museum, only we should insist that the museum should not obtrude into the workshop and that we should not get the two things mixed up.

One suggestion I have heard, which I am inclined to favour, is that Shell should be asked to remove to Glasgow like the Post Office Savings Bank, or to Newcastle like the Ministry of Pensions, which is in line with the policy of two Governments to redistribute industry to Scotland and the North. The House of Commons could then move in, leaving the House of Lords where it is.

When a foreign visitor looks across the river and sees the magnificent white skyscraper towering over the building that houses the Government of Greater London he is apt to come to the conclusion that it is Shell Oil that is the most powerful of British institutions, and he may not be far wrong.

An enormous amount of money must have been spent on re-patching and renovating the ancient fabric of the Palace of

Westminster in a make-do and mend policy which would have gone a long way to providing a magnificent building of which Britain and the Commonwealth might well be proud. After all it would have cost a quarter of the sum spent on an aircraft carrier or the third of the Polaris submarine, which will be obsolete before the time that it is completed.

However, when one thinks of the people who are living in overcrowded rooms within a mile of Westminster, we are entitled to give some consideration to the plight of our neighbours before embarking on anything on the grandoise scale. Rebuilding Westminster should not be one of the priorities until we have broken the back of the housing problem and given the country the schools, the universities and the hospitals it so much needs.

CHAPTER 16

HOW CHURCHILL WOULD HAVE REFORMED PARLIAMENT

Sir Winston Churchill showed his respect and affection for the House of Commons by remaining there as a Member until he was ninety and resolutely declining to depart in peace to the mausoleum of the House of Lords about which in his younger days he had spoken with such contempt.

But he did not think the House of Commons was a perfect institution and had his own very definite ideas of how it should be reformed and modernized and outlined them in the evidence he gave before the Select Committee on Procedure that sat in 1931. Ramsay Macdonald's second Labour Government was in office and it was a time when there was a good deal of public interest in what was happening in Parliament.

The Liberals held the balance at Westminster and were demanding electoral reform which would have given them a greater representation in the House and were also pressing for changes in the procedure of the House itself. There had also arrived at Westminster many new Labour M.P.s who had served on the local authorities and found Parliamentary procedure hopelessly behind the times.

The Select Committee that was set up in 1931 certainly took a great deal of trouble to hear evidence from all quarters. It summoned before it the Prime Minister, Ramsay Macdonald, and two ex-Prime Ministers, Lloyd George and Stanley Baldwin, and a galaxy of politicians from all parties, whips and old Members ranging from Earl Winterton to Sir Oswald Mosley.

The Select Committee had certainly a very large variety of evidence on which it could have produced some interesting recommendations. It was presided over by Mr Ernest Brown, a Liberal whom the Committee elected against Mr Rhys Davies (Labour). On the Committee were six Labour M.P.s, six Conservatives and three Liberals, so it is little wonder that it did not arrive at any agreed conclusions except ultimately in October to report that 'at this late period in the session it is not in their power to complete their Report', and by that time the Labour Government was no longer in power.

The evidence and the examination of the witnesses was however extremely interesting. Re-reading this Report of 1931 one is struck by the fact that the questions that were asked and the issues raised were almost the same that one finds in the Report of the 1965 Procedure Committee. Thirty-four years had gone by but the parliamentary procedure had not greatly changed.

Churchill had not then been Prime Minister but he had been Chancellor of the Exchequer under the Baldwin administration and had been one of the most prominent personalities in politics for the previous twenty-five years.

The first question that was put to him by the chairman was:

'You will have noticed that there are two problems; the first is as to whether any radical reform of the whole system is required, and if not, what views you have with regard to reforming in detail?'

Churchill replied:

'I am in favour, as perhaps is known, of very considerable changes in the direction of devolution to local bodies, much larger in scale than any that exist, or almost any that exist, in the country at the present time. I am also in favour of what is called an Economic Sub Parliament being formed which would guide and aid Parliament in all commercial business and financial questions, or at any rate on many of them; but I consider both of these subjects as too large and too speculative to be treated of in my evidence before this Committee. I merely put them forward in order to put them on one side.'

The Committee, however, decided that Churchill's proposals were in the terms of its remit, even if they meant constitutional changes, but that his proposals for an Economic Sub Parliament could be considered at another session.

He then proceeded to make a few remarks which expressed in general terms his views on Parliament, saying:

'I am very much in favour of the House obtaining more control over its own business from day to day. I am very much in favour of greater flexibility. There is nothing new in this, it is recalling the old vanished liberties and flexibilities of the past. As you know, the

House of Commons, a hundred years ago, debated whatever it wanted to debate and whatever the country wanted it to debate pretty well when it liked. Petitions were presented at the beginning of business, and on these petitions, if the House were in the mood and there was a feeling that the matter should be discussed, debate arose. That was an immense flexibility of procedure. After all, if this House is to maintain its vitality and its hold on the public interest, it must discuss the burning issues of the day, and it must discuss them in great debates. At the present time it seems to me we are too much encumbered with routine. An immense amount of routine is imposed upon the House, and all these routine steps are taken, not *pro formo*, as they might well be unless they raised some important question of principle, but they are taken probably one after the other, and so you find the House sitting at inordinate lengths and consuming the months in a series of chopped up and petty discussions on this subject and that.

'With the preface that my remarks are of a general character, I would say that the whole principle which I advocate would be to confine, to the end of the day, as it were, it being understood that the Government got their business each day, because the routine business must be disposed of. The result of that would be that you would have the main hours of the sitting free for Parliament to debate the great topics of public interest and to debate them continuously, if it felt inclined, day after day.

'Take the question of unemployment as a typical question. I suppose we must have spent twenty days discussing it in the last year [in that year there were over a million unemployed]. Has any good come out of it at all? Every debate has been detached from the other, has been discursive and disconnected and has just come to a useless, futile conclusion. Supposing the House had really addressed itself to this immense problem, resolved to follow it up and pursue it from point to point adopting the old method of resolution, descending from the general to the particular, and taking the conclusions and opinions at each stage, and the agreements at each stage; it is inconceivable to me that we should not have arrived at some conclusions among ourselves and that we should not have guided the opinion of the country.'

Mr Hore-Belisha: Would you meet the criticism that is made outside, that there is too much talk here, by saying that there should be more opportunities for talk on the bigger issues and less for talk on the smaller ones?

Churchill: Yes. If I might come to detail for a moment. I would therefore like to lighten the routine work of the House of Commons, and give the House more power to debate general topics when it wished. I should like to restore some of the old flexibility which has disappeared in the twentieth century and at the end of the nineteenth century. I cannot maintain to have made an exhaustive survey, but I have looked first of all (having lived nearly all my life here) to the debates on Supply and to the debates on Supplementary Estimates. I consider the debates on Supplementary Estimates are the most worthless I have known in my career. They deal with comparatively small sums of money, that is small compared to the national budget, and yet often five or six days are consumed in these debates. There I am sure you could find an economy of time. Then there is the question of the Supply Days, which, of course, furnish convenient pegs for hanging discussions upon. If the House had more power to bring up general discussions of any topics, whenever it wished, in my opinion it would not be so necessary to have the full number of Supply Days, or if these Supply Days were used for general discussion, it being understood that the Supply went through at the end of the day, then there would not be the same necessity to ask for repeated votes of censure as occurs now, and consequently you would have more time. Now what do we want to economize time for? I suggest a very good object; it is to clear the House of routine and cut down the number of days spent on routine, not to pass more legislation, because the amount of legislation the country can take in a session is pretty well fixed, but we want to abridge the sittings of Parliament. If you wish to say what is wrong with Parliament, it is that it sits far too long in the year. I would lay it down that except in times of war or on great national emergency Parliament should not sit for more than five months, with the ordinary short intervals, say, occupying six months of the year. That ought to be the maximum.'

Churchill certainly did not want M.P.s overworked. But with all the demands for more legislation the British electorate in 1965 would take a poor view of M.P.s who were only at Westminster for six months of the year. Questions would undoubtedly be asked, and justifiably so, what they were doing to earn their money, especially with the salary having gone up to £3,250 a year, the Lawrence Committee that recommended it acting on the assumption that Membership of Parliament is a full-time job. Churchill defended his idea on the ground that thirty years before, Parliament only sat for six months in a year. That, however, was in the 1880s and the problems that Parliament has to deal with today are much greater and more complex than they were then. Churchill, however, longed for the more leisurely days, defending it by saying:

'In the intervals Ministers are able to study their work, discussions can take place on the platform outside, a lot of foolish ideas are ventilated, passion is aroused and so on; and then when Parliament meets again everyone is delighted and they say "It is high time

K

Parliament met and there is keen attention in all parts of the country, everyone bursting to have his grievance redressed and so on. As things are at present you get the King's Speech and the opening debates on the address, and no one can distinguish those from the rest of the business which dribbles out in a dreary stream through the rest of the year. There is no feature: you cannot hold the attention of the more democratic electorate unless there is something definite done, something to be discussed at set times and on great occasions. Therefore I suggest that everything possible should be done to lighten the routine work of Parliament into at least one half of the year and that will leave time in which a democratic Chamber will be able to fortify its hold on public opinion.'

When he was asked by the Rev. James Barr, a Scots Labour M.P. who had introduced a Home Rule for Scotland Bill, 'Do you think some measure of relief might come in the way of shortening the session if we had a measure of devolution for Wales and Scotland and so on?' he replied 'Yes, I do; and if later on you wish me to give evidence upon that I will do so, but I could not do justice to the topic without carefully marshalling my arguments.'

Churchill was in favour of committees that would be able to conduct a more careful scrutiny of public expenditure. Replying to a question on that point he said:

'I think you will find it very difficult to break in on the responsibilities of Ministers and of the Executive to present their Departments' Estimates as a whole. I agree that after they have been presented to Parliament their consideration should take place by committees dealing with each branch, Military, Civil and so forth, and that these Committees should apply the scrutiny which the public imagine is applied on Supply Days, but which has fallen into very great disuse. I should be in favour of the Estimates for the current year going up to be criticized and examined in a series of committees — quite small committees too — and that these committees should report to the House. They would make a report, for instance, on the Army Estimates, or on the Naval Estimates or the Civil Service Estimates—they would make a report and the Estimate would come before the House with a report drawing attention to all that could be said about it, and any weak points or scandals that had come to light, or any means of making revisions would be placed before the House before the subject is debated on Supply Day.'

He stressed this in a reply to a later question.

'When the Army Estimate comes out, it should go straight away to a committee composed of less members than there are on this committee and they should be able to send for the Minister and to send for the officials and ask them questions, just in the same way as the Public Accounts Committee do today.'

So that in this respect Churchill in 1931 was advocating giving more powers to committees for the purpose that we are arguing today.

He stressed the point again when he was asked if the House would be more chary of losing the opportunity of criticizing the Estimates if it were short of time.

'I think the House would gain more in being able to criticize exactly the points it wished, and as I say, the procedure would be that the Estimate would come before the House—a great fat book—with a Report pinned on to it, attached to it by a committee which would say "Look here, this is very wrong; see this, notice how this is increasing; this is a scandal; we ought to have more information about this, the Secretary for the Post Office gave us in evidence the following" and so on, and the House would say "Hullo, here we are now we must have a field day about this, coming on two days later, look here the 'War Office' or 'The Admiralty' or whatever it is 'they are exposed' "; then there would be a very keen debate and the Government would have to fight for its life—as every Government ought.'

The case for committee examination of Government expenditure could hardly have been put better than that. Churchill did not mention the Air Estimates, for at that time they were not as large as the others. Between 1951 and 1964 it was the Air Estimates that needed the closest scrutiny. The Estimates and the Public Accounts Committee did succeed in drawing attention to some of the worst scandals. But if the procedure that Churchill had suggested had been in operation they might have been discovered earlier. Churchill suggested that the Minister responsible, as well as the civil servants, should appear before the examining committee. Close and detailed scrutiny upstairs, leaving the floor of the House for the more general debates, was the theme of what Churchill advocated, and later experience has certainly confirmed that he was right.

Mr Rhys Davies asked him:

'I take it that you are firmly of the opinion that the parliamentary system is the best still?'

'Yes, the least intolerable of any form of government yet.'

'You are rather inclined to the view that the House of Commons should be a greater centre for debate. I take it you mean that it ought to devote itself more to oratory than at present? Do you suggest that we should go to the rostrum that they have got in other Parliaments?'

'No. I am entirely opposed to any alteration in the architectural lay-out of the Chamber or of the arrangement.'

'But the tendency, surely, if Parliament accepted your view, would be that the debate in the House of Commons would be confined to a very few Members of Parliament. Is that not so?'

'Oh, no.'

'You cannot have oratory without an orator, can you?'

'I have never used the word oratory at all. It does not follow that flowery speeches are the best method of threshing out subjejcts; it is quite conceivable that the speeches would be short and ruggedly simple, but the point I am on is that there should be more continuity, more pursuing of subjects to a definite conclusion than there is now.'

'Do you think that the character of legislation has changed? Do you think that all these insurance schemes, taking the time of Parliament, have altered the debating quality in the House of Commons?'

'No, but where there are great masses of detail they ought to be dealt with by competent committees.'

'You would not get a very important speech on the details of Unemployment Insurance or National Insurance, would you?'

'I should have thought so. I should have thought there were issues connected with both of these which might well have been focused and threshed out by Parliament in a very lengthy debate extending over many days.'

'National Health Insurance?'

'National Health Insurance certainly raises issues which are well deserving of being lifted to the very centre of the stage for a day or two.'

Churchill stuck to his idea that Parliament should not meet more than five or six months a year when he was questioned by Sir Hugh O'Neill. 'I think we kill Parliament', he repeated, 'by going on practically without intermission. I think we kill it.'

Sir Hugh O'Neill: Do you think the one difficulty today as compared with former times in making the House sit only five or six months in the year is that the Members are now paid? Do you think that makes a difference?

'No.'

'You do not think there would be a tendency on the part of people to say "These fellows are now paid; they are public servants getting salaries, they have jolly well got to do some work"?'

Sir Hugh O'Neill knew his fellow countryman better than Churchill did, but Churchill replied:

'At any rate it would be the wrong way of looking at it.'

Sir Hugh pursued the point:

'But you have heard a complaint made by Members inside the House, when we have been rising in August, that we ought not to be rising because of unemployment?'
'Of course they may have said that, but broadly speaking, I do not think the fact that Members are paid would influence me on this point. They should not be paid on the quantity of their work but for the quality of their work. A Member may earn his salary a dozen times over by a very few judicious reflections contributed to our general knowledge. It has not to be looked on as a treadmill which has to be turned so many times to earn the screw.'
'I quite agree, but do you not think it is a rather widely held view in the country?'
'It is a view that should be corrected by a vigorous race of parliamentarians.'

Repeated questions did not succeed in making Churchill budge from his point of view and he repeated later, 'No, I am sure it makes a tremendous difference to the good government of this country to have five or six months when Parliament is not sitting'.
The most frequent objection to the setting up of committees is that Ministers and civil servants would object to them. Sir Hugh O'Neill put this to Churchill.

'I take it, as Chancellor of the Exchequer, as you were in the last Government, you would have welcomed some such procedure of that kind for giving the House power to discuss expenditure?'
'Yes, certainly.'
'Because it is, after all, one of the main objects of the Chancellor of the Exchequer to reduce expenditure—is it not?'
'I would welcome it as a Minister of a spending Department. I have been head of several spending Departments and I would always be ready to go before a committee and explain fully to them why things had cost so much or why we should not do it cheaper or whatever it was. I would be glad to be cross-examined by a committee, I do not think any Minister should shrink from that.'

A further answer to Sir Hugh O'Neill reveals how Churchill in 1931 knew the objections to the committee system he advocated and they are precisely the same as we hear today.

Sir Hugh O'Neill: What you have in your mind, obviously, is something much more thorough than the present Estimates Committee—small committees of half a dozen or ten which would really go into the Departments if necessary and have power to examine any official of any Department?

'Everything must be covered by the ministerial responsibility. The official may say "My Secretary of State has not authorized me to answer that question". Then if the committee are angry with that they must carry that complaint to the House, and the House has to settle with the Government, but the Government will probably have a majority to support the Minister. But that is perfectly all right; it would work out in nine cases out of ten. I think in fact much more.'

'That is one of the great troubles as to how far you would let these committees make recommendations to reduce expenditure which depended upon policy?'

'I think there is not the slightest reason why they should not make recommendations for reduced expenditure. I would not allow them to make recommendations for increased expenditure, following the principle which prevails in the House. They cannot settle it, but let us be told what we ought to do in the House, let us have the advice certainly.'

Winston Churchill had certainly given the Select Committee on Procedure something to think about and he returned on June 14th with a memorandum in which he advocated an Economic Sub Parliament.

It certainly showed that while Churchill had a great respect almost amounting to veneration for the traditions of the House of Commons and for the British Constitution, he was not afraid of innovations.

The memorandum was certainly a big morsel to ask the Mother of Parliaments to swallow.

'Parliament would be well advised', it declared, 'to create a new assembly, subordinate to itself, free from organized party exigencies, detached from public opinion and composed of persons possessing special qualifications in economic and commercial matters. The German constitution has a provision of this kind. Evidently the composition, powers and procedure of this body are details about which opinion will vary. I should tentatively suggest that the Economic Sub Parliament be set up by statute and should consist of 120 members, of whom 40 would be Members of the House of Commons experienced in these subjects and 80 business men, trade union representatives or economic authorities. The whole 120 would be chosen in proportion to the strength of parties of the House of Commons by the leaders of parties, it being the acknowledged duty of such leaders to consider first of all the character and efficiency of the new assembly. Among those chosen there would be not less than twenty members of the House of Lords. The terms of membership would be three years without regard to the date of general elections.'

This certainly was a new body to be grafted on to the British Constitution and to which it seemed Parliament was being asked to sub-let as it were some of its powers or duties.

For Churchill went on to propose that all Bills, after having been read the second time by either House, dealing with trade and industry would be automatically referred to the Economic Sub Parliament, unless the House where the Bill originated determined otherwise.

Members of the Select Committee gave the proposal a rather frosty reception and Churchill was not nearly so confident about it as he had been in outlining his ideas on the previous occasion. He admitted that in effect any Bill dealing with trade and industry would be remitted to the Economic Sub Parliament for what would be a second reading, thus side-tracking the House of Commons, though in the final stage the Bill would be subject to the decision of Parliament and so Parliament would retain its supreme authority.

Nobody could seriously argue that the Economic Sub Parliament would be by any stretch of imagination a democratic body. It would not even be chosen by Parliament but by the party leaders.

Churchill's argument was that it would take industrial and trade matters out of the atmosphere of party politics. In one of his answers to a question why such a new body was necessary he replied:

'Primarily it is to achieve what is not now achieved in our polity, namely a tense, constructive discussion of economic and commercial issues that is not now taking place at Westminster and has not for a great many years. There has been no clear, tense discussion of economic issues here that I have heard—certainly nothing adequate. Political issues are very well dealt with, and the House acts admirably as a college from which the choice of Ministers can be made and it acts as the foundation of the Executive—but as far as finding out what is the best thing for us to do in the financial, currency or economic question, I do not think it is adequate at the present time and it might well strengthen itself by adding the new element. That is my basic thought.'

The answer was about as damning an indictment of the British Parliament as could have been made. For if Parliament was inadequate to deal with economic problems and needed to send out an SOS to some Economic Sub Parliament to come to its rescue it must have been in a bad way indeed. What Churchill was advocating was really a grafting on of Mussolini's Fascist Corporate State to the British Constitution. Parliament was in effect being asked to recognize that in facing the economic problems of the time it would not do its job. There was a good deal of admiration of Mussolini in Western European Governments at the time and Churchill himself, when Chancellor of the Exchequer in January 1927, had gone to Rome where he had eulogized Italian Fascism and had declared publicly to Mussolini, 'If I had been an Italian, I am sure that I should have been with you wholeheartedly from start to finish in your triumphant struggle against the bestial habits and passions of Leninism'. There was not much democracy about this and in later years Churchill must have been thankful that he was *not* born an Italian.

Churchill was a skilful and colourful parliamentarian but the Economic Sub Parliament was not one of his happiest suggestions for improving Parliament. It was stillborn and was soon buried, and soon Churchill became more preoccupied with other things. He did not revive the idea in later years, probably because he realized that it was better forgotten, like his flirtation with Mussolini.

CHAPTER 17

LLOYD GEORGE'S IDEAS

Lloyd George expressed the view in his evidence before the 1931 Select Committee on Procedure that the influence of Parliament had declined in his time. He was the Father of the House, was there about forty years and had been Prime Minister and so was in a position to know. He recognized there was a good deal of criticism of Parliamentary institutions and a great and growing disappointment with Parliament. He thought there was 'a growing feeling that Parliament was not coping with its task and not altogether discharging the trust which the nation had reposed in it'.

He stated that apart from Votes of Censure debates or at moments of great political excitement the general attendance at the House was less than five per cent of its membership and that this gave 'the impression that the House of Commons is only concerned about the political game and not at all about the real business of the nation'.

He went on:

'If I am asked what was responsible for the slackness I come straight to the question of procedure. It was not that there was not a great deal of interest on the part of Members in this vital question (unemployment) but because they felt these discussions would lead nowhere. You could not carry things any further merely by these broad discussions. The House of Commons has no machinery, or at least it has not set up any machinery for pursuing the subject in the practical details and for investigating these questions closely . . . The House of Commons has no committees at the present moment to which these all-important matters can be referred. The fact of the matter is that the House has no real effective and continuous control over the actions of the Executive. Every municipality in the land has committees which consider every important detail of administration and report on it to the council. The general discussions take place there. The examination in detail takes place in the committees which are set up for that purpose. You have a finance committee, a public works committee, a police committee and a health committee and there are all kinds of committees. On questions of principle you have a debate in the council chamber, but the close examination takes place in committees where the officials are present and questions can be put to them, and, if the committee would like to have any outside opinion, if they think any other opinion would enlighten them upon the topics they are examining, they can send for anybody. But you have no kind of machinery of that kind in the House of Commons and until you have it, the House of Commons will have no effective control over the Executive.'

'Of course that would apply to administrative things but not so much to legislation?'

'Well, it might. For instance it might lead to recommendations in favour of legislative improvements. For instance a suggestion might be made and the Minister would say "You cannot do this without legislation" and if a committee came to the conclusion that it was desirable that that should be done then recommendations could be made under that particular heading. I do not think these committees are confined to mere administration.'

'Are you thinking of large committees or small ones?'

'Comparatively small. I think a large committee is not an effective business body. About the size of this one (fifteen).'

In reply to further questions Lloyd George went on to say that he did not want the committee to control Departmental Affairs in regard to administration.

'The control must rest with the Minister because he is responsible to Parliament and through Parliament to the Crown. The Minister must have the ultimate say, subject to what Parliament says, but it would enable the House of Commons effectively to supervise and not only that but to keep itself informed.'

'Do you envisage the Minister being chairman of such a committee?'

'No, the Minister is in the House.'

'He is summoned before the committee?'

'Yes, he comes before the committee.'

'And a civil servant might also be examined?'

'Certainly. I would suggest you would have power to send for anybody and no information could be withheld?'

'Oh no.'

In his evidence Lloyd George was emphatic in his argument that the municipal committee system should be adapted to Parliament. He thought that our municipal procedure was an admirable one. He had been campaigning in the Press for his ideas and was cross-examined on them by Mr Hacking. One of the articles he had written to the *Daily Express* had begun with the sentence 'Parliamentary institutions are on their trial'.

'Do you adhere to that?' asked Mr Hacking (a Conservative whip).

'I do very much so,' replied Lloyd George.

'Is a Parliament such as we have here now on trial?'

'Yes, that is right.'

'You continued "Parliament must be rationalized if it is to do its work well or even do it at all"?'

'That is right.'

'And this is the form of rationalization you would suggest?'

'That is one suggestion I certainly would make. I think Parliament is an antiquated machine and it certainly needs rationalization to make it effective.'

'And this is the main form of rationalization?'

'That is one suggestion.'

Lloyd George held that the committee system would be good for Ministers. He explained:

'There is nothing under our present system of procedure to stop a Government setting up a committee to go into telephones and to report to it?'

'Yes, but you cannot expect a Minister to create embarrassments for himself by supporting special committees, I will not say to help him but to harass him; but once he knows that he has got to go through this mill and that he has got to face a committee which will gradually get to know the job—even if it does not at the start—because people get, as they do on municipalities, to know the whole thing from beginning to end, and there are some men who work very hard at it and get to know just as much as the Minister does, and very often probably more—with due respect to the Minister—when he knows that he has to face committees of that kind it would do him good—and the officials too.'

Lloyd George knew all the arguments and the answers and he had the advantage of other witnesses because he had been a member for many years of a county council and knew exactly how the procedure he was advocating for Parliament worked.

He dismissed the idea that Parliament controlled the Executive as 'pure fiction' and he argued that the responsibility for government should not be shirked by individual M.P.s.

When the question was put to him whether he was not throwing too great a responsibility on Members he retorted:

'You have 600 men who are responsible for a great country under the greatest Empire in the world. And my view is that they *ought* to take a definite responsibility and that each individual Member ought to feel that he has a share of that responsibility. His general attitude of mind now is either to leave it to the Government of the day if he is supporting it, or, if he is opposing to say so in Parliament or on the platform, but in a committee system each Member would have a kind of responsibility of his own for some part of the work of governing.'

I doubt if anyone has ever put the case for a committee system of government more clearly and forcibly than Lloyd George did in his evidence before the 1931 Committee on Procedure.

But the fact that we are still asking the same questions in 1966 that he answered so effectively then shows how strong the forces of tradition and conservatism are in the British House of Commons. Lloyd George, of course, put his finger on the spot when he referred to the opposition of Ministers to have committees examining what is going on in their Departments. There are the weak Ministers, the stronger ones like Lloyd George and Churchill had no objection. But a really strong Parliament would show its determination by insisting that they were the servants of Parliament and that Parliament was not theirs. How many of us have not seen at one time or another that the figure reading his departmental briefs at the dispatch box is not really a responsible Minister at all but a reader out of the views of some civil servant who is really running the show!

A first-class Minister would have no objections to co-operating with a committee of M.P.s, for they are all there as representatives of the people and all M.P.s are equal at election times. What weak Ministers fear is that the members of the committee will soon get to know more about the Department than they do. Too often one has sensed that the Minister and the civil servants in the box are really a conspiracy against Parliament. That is why Parliament should always be vigilant in scrutinizing what is being done. That is what M.P.s should be at Westminster for.

Let us look at it from the reverse point of view. What sort of local government would we get in our cities or in our councils if the chairmen were to select their nominees to run the different departments and if there were no committees?

Committees would also be good training grounds for potential

Ministers. Too often now Ministers are placed in their particular jobs not because they have had experience or have knowledge of the problems that have to be faced there but because they have been prominent in political activities and whom the Prime Minister of the day thinks it necessary to reward for their support and loyalty in some pre-election situation or on the other hand as potential opponents whom it is wise to conciliate and placate.

In any well run local authority the chairman, the chairmen of committees, committee members and officials do not look upon each other suspiciously as natural enemies but as men and women working together for the common good. Why should not civil servants, Ministers and M.P.s at Westminster work together in the same way?

CHAPTER 18

MUNICIPALIZE PARLIAMENT?

A new type of Labour M.P. began to arrive in Parliament after 1906. These were the men who had served their apprenticeship to government on the local authorities. There they had been advocating the application of the principles of municipal socialism fighting for a more human administration of the poor law, for such things as the feeding of schoolchildren, better schools for the working-class children, for the removal of the slums and municipal housing, and the improvement of the social services which the local authorities controlled. They were used to a world of town clerks and treasurers, sanitary inspectors and road surveyors and directors of education, with whom they came in regular contact and whose reports they discussed at their committee and sub-committee meetings. They knew that the detailed and constructive work of local government was done round the table where party politics did not always operate and where those who were persistent and knew the facts could get concessions and achieve results even when they were in minorities. These they could get to know exactly how much money was being spent and how much more needed to be if the life of a town or county or a parish was to be run efficiently, intelligently and humanly.

But when they arrived at Westminster it was all so different. Here they found themselves remote from the real problems with which they had been accustomed to deal in their local authority life, never meeting the civil servants, with a parliamentary procedure which tended to make them mere political robots and puppets of the party machine, often having to vote in ways which they felt were wrong just because the recognized thing was to vote on party lines either in order to keep a Government in power or to defeat it, waiting for division bells to be duly shepherded into lobbies, directed by the whips, often with very little idea of what it was all about. The old type of M.P. saw nothing wrong with this, this was what had been happening there for generations, what their grandfathers and fathers had done before them, this was the Mother of Parliaments, the glorious British Constitution in operation, the most wonderful method of government, going on from precedent to precedent, that divine providence had ever created.

Many of them accepted it and adapted themselves to it. They had gone to Westminster to capture it but before long Westminster had captured them.

There were some however who said 'We are living in the twentieth century and we have enormous social problems to face. How can it ever be done if we do not alter the procedure in this place and turn it into a workshop instead of a mere talking shop?'

Among these Members was Fred W. Jowett of Bradford, who had been playing an active and notable part in the local politics of his native town. Nobody less like Gladstone or Winston Churchill could have been imagined. He had no time for any of the parliamentary traditions that wasted people's time and he regarded conventional Westminster oratory as Henry Ford regarded conventional history as bunk, and he turned his considerable critical faculties at the way they did things in the House of Commons and asked the scandalous question why the Mother of Parliaments couldn't run its business as intelligently and as sensibly as the Bradford Town Council. For over twenty years in the Press, on the platform, at the party conferences and in the House of Commons itself he carried on a persistent campaign for his ideas of running Parliament on different lines. He had innumerable arguments and controversies with Ramsay Macdonald, who was hypnotized by Parliament and became one of its principal spellbinders although this did prevent Macdonald from recognizing his abilities and his knowledge of local government and making him the Minister of Works in his first Cabinet.

Both Ramsay Macdonald and Jowett gave evidence before the 1931 Select Committee on Procedure and it was in striking contrast. Macdonald always had a habit of resenting criticism and talking in superior terms of condescension towards his critics, especially if he suspected that they might be right.

He began his evidence by a sweeping condemnation of those who were demanding changes in the procedure of Parliament.

'I have read a good deal about new Parliaments, created, some at the fireside, and some from the municipal council, and some from people who have been here. I have not come across a single, what I call fireside construction, that I believe will bear practical examination, not one. From the point of view of those who have come into this House with municipal experience, which is characteristically committee experience, I do not think that a legislature such as this can be modelled on that system at all. An administrative local body can only act in accordance with its powers and is restricted accordingly in dealing with large policy. If you are going to have a machine adapted for the purpose that it is supposed to serve, you must not model a legislature like this upon a municipal administrative body. That is generally what I would say. Then, regarding certain proposals that have been made by men who have been here and who have seen some of our defects, I should like to ask the committee to examine such proposals as are made on the assumption that the spirit in which we do our work here will be carried on under the new proposals.'

Macdonald had by this time reached the stage when he took refuge in a cloud of nebulosities. This became more and more obvious as he went on:

'A parliamentary machine is rather like a living organism, you have to balance up rights and wrongs.'

It was very difficult to have a rational argument with anybody who talked like that.

When he was asked the direct question by Sir Basil Peto

'All I want to be clear about is, do you shut out altogether the idea of dividing your Parliament into different committees on county council lines?"

he replied:

'No, what I would do is this. If you are considering how to reform the machinery of this House so that the House may become more efficient, I do not think you can do so on these lines. I do not think you can do it on these principles. If we were discussing here whether it would not be advisable to create what one might call advisory committees on these subjects, that is a matter on which my mind is far more open than it is on the other subject.'

Macdonald seemed to have conceded a good deal of the argument.

When he was asked 'There is no way of giving the Back Bencher any sense of responsibility?' he replied 'Unless interviewing them occasionally by their Leader will do it'.

Macdonald did appear to realize that there was something wrong with the House of Commons but he did not quite know what to do about it. He said later:

'I am not so much interested in the rapidity of business getting through as in the lopping off of waste time, because I see such a lot of waste of time in the House. We should not shut our eyes to that. One of the great troubles in getting these benches on both sides of the House well filled all through is that you go and see Members sitting reading and writing and say "Why are not you in the Chamber?" and they say "It is a waste of time". We can never cure that but if all parties in the House lay their heads together, I think we could cure a great deal of it.'

Before the year was out Macdonald and his Conservative opponents had 'put their heads together', but it was to form a Coalition Government and whatever it did, it did not end the waste of time in the House. Then M.P.s did less and the benches were emptier than ever.

When Jowett came to give evidence he was as definite as Macdonald was woolly. He certainly said what he would do and argued the case for it in his examination before the committee.

What he wanted was parliamentary business organized on municipal lines as much as possible. Jowett had clearly given more thought to the question than anybody else who gave evidence before the 1931 Committee and his proposals would have drastically changed the procedure of Parliament. He could have had little hope that a Government with Ramsay Macdonald at its head would consider them seriously. Indeed they are perhaps too drastic and thoroughgoing for the Parliamentary reformers of today and certainly for M.P.s who have adapted themselves to the old traditions. But Jowett did know what was wrong with the House of Commons and many of his ideas will have to be accepted if Parliament is to adapt its procedure to meet the conditions of today and the future.

Jowett was a prolific writer on the subject and continued his campaign when he was no longer in Parliament. He succeeded ultimately in converting the Independent Labour Party to his ideas and it published his summary of his proposals in a

L

pamphlet *Parliament and Palaver*[1] in which he replied in detail to his critics, especially Ramsay Macdonald, who had argued that Socialism could never be established in Britain if we adopted the committee system in our Government.

He worked out in detail how a Land Nationalization Bill could be passed through the House of Commons more easily under the committee system.

He ended his pamphlet with the assertion:

'Parliament cannot for long be maintained as the governing body in this country if it is not made the instrument by which representative government is carried on, in fact as well as by repute. Used as it is now to stifle initiative and difference of opinion honestly held, and to give the least possible opening for new measures and policies, Parliament invites attack alike from camouflaged enemies of the people, who would make it permanently their wash-pot, and from the revolutionaries who seek to establish dictatorship on its ruins. We consider, therefore, that the Labour Party, at the first opportunity, will apply the method and practice of representative government in Parliament.'

And those words might well be pondered over by the Labour Party of today.

---

[1] See the Memorandum in the Appendix.

CHAPTER 19

SHAW ON THE PARTY SYSTEM

Bernard Shaw wrote a good deal about the need for reforming Parliament. In both of his political text books, *The Intelligent Woman's Guide to Socialism* and *Everybody's Political What's What*, he described how the Party System had originated in King William's deciding, on the advice of the Earl of Sunderland, to choose his Ministers from one party only, so as to get Parliament to grant him the money for his wars with France. In the later book he wrote in dialogue form a dialogue between King William and Sunderland explaining how it came about. In the earlier book he wrote:

'The party system was introduced because our Dutch King William the Third, of glorious, pious and immortal memory, discovered that he could not fight the French King, Louis XIV, with a House of Commons refusing him supplies and reducing the army just as each Member thought fit. A clever statesman of that time named Robert Spencer pointed out to him that if he chose his Ministers always from the strongest party in the House of Commons, which happened just then to be the Whig party, that party would have to back him throughout the war and make its followers do the same. King William hated the Whigs, being a strong Tory himself; and he did not like Sunderland's advice. But he took it and thus set up the system under which we are ruled.'

Shaw came to the conclusion that the result of this in the twentieth century is that 'the two Houses of Parliament are as much out of date as instruments for carrying on the public business of a modern community as a pair of horses for drawing a modern bus'.

He was always arguing that the municipal system of government was infinitely preferable to what was going on in the House of Commons.

Shaw had himself in his younger days been a very conscientious member of the St Pancras Borough Council which later gave him its freedom. He stood for the London County Council but was unsuccessful because of the independent line he persisted in taking and his determination not to compromise in any way with any section of the electorate. Indeed at one time, so the letters of Mrs Shaw revealed, the possibility of him fighting at a General Election for what was considered a safe Labour seat was considered, but it did not materialize.

Shaw thought that the Party System as it worked at Westminster had the effect of extinguishing, demoralizing or destroying the influence of those that went there.

When John Burns died in January 1943 he wrote an article to *Forward* entitled 'The Lesson of Burns and Lloyd George'. He wrote:

'I wish Lloyd George would write another book. He was good natured enough to tell the House of Commons that there is nothing that he is prouder of than the fifty-three years he has spent in it. This remark has struck John Burns dead. For he also made his way from the candle factory in which he worked as a boy to sway multitudes as The Man with the Red Flag and the heroic orator of the great strike for the dockers' tanner, formidable enough to be made the first proletarian to sit on the Treasury bench as a Cabinet Minister. Nothing less could have extinguished him.

'After Bloody Sunday in Trafalgar Square Burns did time for six weeks, his captivity being shared by Cunninghame Graham. Graham, a thoroughbred aristocrat, never sat on the Treasury bench. He damned the House's hypocrisy to its face and shook its dust from his feet. Had he stayed there and played the Party game he would have shared the fate of Burns and Lloyd George . . . Were these the only volcanoes that our parliamentary system extinguished?

'Take John Stuart Mill and Sidney Webb. Who has ever had a word to say against their good faith, public spirit, extraordinary knowledge and first-rate ability? But the time they spent in Parliament and in getting there was so utterly wasted that they were glad to go home to their proper work and stay there.

'Webb presented the seat he had made safe to Macdonald, who having begun as the most intransigent of Socialists out of Parliament in it became such a complete do-nothing bunk merchant that he was made Prime Minister and was cherished by the Conservatives until they found they could do without him as well as, or better than with him, after which he died in what was called prominent neglect.

'Keir Hardie kept the faith but he could do nothing with the House and died bewildered by its futility and his own. Smillie, great until he became M.P., was hardly noticed there.

'Bradlaugh was hated and dreaded so much by the governing class that he was thrown down the stairs at Westminster when he was elected and attempted to take his seat. It took six policemen to do it and his struggle with them shortened his life, but he came back to help the Government with a long overdue Truck Act and then to subside as a quiet anti-Socialist Member and die. Hilaire Belloc just took the measure of the place, spat at it and left it. Maxton is still wasting his life there, making no legislative difference by his presence and entertaining the heavily bored Members by his gifts as a speaker. I could multiply examples, but enough is enough. The men to head Governments there are the men who can be trusted to do nothing like Baldwin and Ramsay.

'Readers will ask how in that case such energetic men of action like Lloyd George and Winston Churchill became Premiers. The answer is that it took two coalition-compelling world wars to do it. Winston had to wait a long time and, like the Welsh wizard, he will be got rid of when the German bayonets are no longer at our throats and the Party System comes back. The truth is that this country is governed not by the House of Commons but partly by the local authorities in which the Party System does not exist (here all the people who do not know what the party system is will contradict me, poor dupes that they are), partly by the bureaucracy, but mostly, as in Russia, by boards, societies, companies, professional associations, trade unions, commissioners, in short miniature Soviets which when they are captured, manned and controlled in the public interest will do here what has been done in Russia . . . I want Lloyd George to write another book contrasting Farmer George of Churt with the Right Honourable hot air artist of Westminster.'

Shaw was not, however, an anti-parliamentary anarchist. What he insisted on was that Parliament must reform itself so that it could be capable of playing its part in bringing about necessary social and economic changes for the transformation of capitalism into a Socialist society. In a chapter in his *Intelligent Woman* called 'Change Must Be Parliamentary' he argued that in spite of everything we 'must resign ourselves, sooner or later, to a parliamentary settlement between the Capitalists and the Socialists'.

'Nothing is ever done and much is prevented', he wrote in the conclusion of this chapter, 'by people who do not realize they cannot do everything at once.'

But he insisted that parliamentary procedure should be changed. He wrote:

'The British Party System should be scrapped ruthlessly. It was invented two and a half centuries ago to nullify the House of Commons by obliging the King to select his Ministers from the party commanding a majority in it and to dissolve Parliament and inflict a costly election on its Members whenever that party is defeated on a division; so that Members never vote on the merits of a measure but always on the question of whether the reigning party is to remain in office, both sides risking the loss of their seats and incurring heavy expense and trouble if they unseat the Government.

'Parliamentary business therefore should be conducted as in our municipalities, where members are elected for a fixed term and serve on standing committees which consider all questions appropriate to their departments and report their conclusions and recommendations to the whole body. The reports can be discussed and accepted or amended or sent back for further consideration on their merits wholly; for no member gains any personal advantage or suffers disadvantage whatever way he votes, nor does the rejection of any recommendation involve an immediate dissolution and election, nor displace the chairman of the reporting committee.'

This is in essence what Jowett advocated too and what the Webbs advocated in their *Constitution for the British Commonwealth*.

Shaw had written so scathingly about Parliament and the fate of well-meaning Socialists who had gone there in the columns of *Forward*, which I had been editing, that it was with some hesitation that I broke the news to him that I had been adopted to fight South Ayrshire at a by-election and inquired if he would send a message.

Back came his reply on a postcard. 'This is the worst news on the Home Front. Another first-rater lured to the talking shop and lost. I am praying daily for your defeat.'

I replied with a postcard of my own and he later sent a long letter commending me to the electors. But I wondered whether he had written me off as another volcano that was on the way to be extinguished at Westminster.

When I went out to see him at Ayot St Lawrence after I had arrived in London he was as doubtful as ever about Parliament and very critical of what the Attlee Government was doing. He asked me to keep in touch with him about what was happening in the House of Commons and I occasionally sent him a copy of Hansard when there was an interesting debate.

Here are his comments on one of the House of Commons debates in March 1949 (he was then over ninety).

Ayot St Lawrence
March 29, 1949

Dear E.H.,

Thanks for the Hansard. I read the Estimate debate as you suggested. It convinced me that the Left Wing should organize its tactics better. Gallacher, who began as one of the best grounded and intelligent of the Communists, is now a tired man, and what is worse, a tiresome man. He is all right for ten minutes and then he drivels off into the commonplaces that were on the spot in 1861 but are now so stale that nobody listens to them, with the result that nobody listens to G. even when he is talking to the point.

Piratin should be reminded of Robert Owen's rule 'Never argue; repeat your assertions'.

On the whole I should recommend a strict Left Wing Rule that no speech should exceed twelve minutes and that no Opposition speaker should be interrupted. Crack debaters love interruptions, they are opportunities. Nothing is more deadly to a speaker than being ignored by silence. Interruptions make a speech sparkle. I am an old hand and I know. A Left Wing of bores is the worst thing that could happen. Add this rule to Owen's, never contradict an opponent: embrace his argument and turn it against him.

G.B.S.

The comment and the advice was very much to the point. The back bencher who makes long speeches is not effective unless he has something unusual to say. They drive out of the House most people—except those who are hopefully waiting to speak next. A time limit of fifteen minutes for a back bencher would improve debates.

Shaw did not think that a Labour Government could be successful in carrying out its policies until it changed parliamentary procedure. In this I thought he took too pessimistic a view of what could be pushed through Parliament by a Government with the kind of majority that Labour was given in 1945. During the five years that followed we did get the Welfare State, and the nationalization of coal, power and transport and many other pieces of legislation which were a substantial instalment of social and economic change. It was after the General Election when Labour had to carry on with a majority of six that one saw how the old procedure could be used against us to delay and obstruct and finally to discredit a Labour Government. But it was not this so much that sent Labour into the wilderness for another thirteen years but the disastrous decision to go into the Korean war, and the big rearmament programme which sent up prices and has been a burden round our necks ever since.

What the Labour Government failed to do in those years was to reform Parliament itself. Herbert Morrison as Leader of the House was as much a Conservative in these matters as anyone. And he has successors today in the Labour Party at Westminster who fail to realise that the modernization of Parliament is an essential step if Britain is to be sensibly governed and to face the difficult problems that we face today.

CHAPTER 20

WHAT IS MUMBO-JUMBO?

It was Mr Turton, the Conservative M.P. for Thirsk and Malton, who brought Mumbo Jumbo into this discussion on Parliament, not me. It was at the sitting of the Committee on Procedure when Dr Horace King, now the Speaker, was giving his evidence. Mr Turton bears a resemblance to Goldie, the Zoo eagle, but like Goldie he has never escaped. Indeed if he had succeeded one fears that they would have recaptured him and brought him back. Since the departure of Sir Winston Churchill and Sir Thomas Moore, Mr Turton has become the Father of the House and having been there for nearly forty years has learned a great deal about its procedure and traditions.

He put a very pertinent question to Dr King.

'Dr King has told us, I think, that he would support any change which could make the procedure of the House more intelligible to the average Member of Parliament, but he qualified that by saying that he thought Members should get themselves fully acquainted with the historical background of the procedure. But is it not as important to try to make our procedure intelligible to the man in the street?'

'Oh yes,' replied Dr King.

Mr Turton: And surely the whole of what we have called the mumbo-jumbo of the Committee of Ways and Means and the Committee of Supply is quite unintelligible to the man-in-the-street or the man in the gallery.

'I would cut out all mumbo-jumbo,' declared Dr King, going on to say that he did not think that the custom of asking for explanations of how the money was to be spent by the Government before voting it was not mumbo-jumbo, an assertion which no one disputes.

'As to the rest of the mumbo-jumbo,' he added later, 'I am sure you are right.'

The Dictionary of Slang defines mumbo-jumbo as 'Meaningless jargon' and 'an object of senseless veneration' which has its origin in Western Africa.

Now there is any amount of mumbo-jumbo to be discarded before we come to the Committee of Ways and Means. Take, for example, what happens before a Bill that has passed through all its other stages receives the Royal Assent. On the last day that the House of Commons met in 1965 I joined the procession that dutifully made its way to the House of Lords for this purpose. It was a debate on the Adjournment of the House during which M.P.s debate a number of different topics.

Among them was a very interesting debate on Television and whether a greater measure of censorship should be exercised over the BBC. Considerable interest had been shown in this question as the result of a certain amount of indignation and disapproval of the use by Mr Kenneth Tynan of an Anglo-Saxon word which when I was in the army I used frequently to see inscribed on the whitewashed walls of Her Majesty's Guard Rooms and was used there not only to express disapproval of military authority but of many other things as well. This had led to a more general discussion of television programmes and what should or what should not be censored. The indignation about Mr Kenneth Tynan seemed to have been especially marked in the City of Birmingham and two of Birmingham's M.P.s, a Labour M.P., Mr Victor Yates, and a Conservative M.P., Mr Dance, had vied with each other in denouncing the BBC.

M.P.s in the Chamber waited curiously to hear what the Postmaster-General wished to say, and Mr Anthony Wedgewood-Benn had obviously prepared a very careful speech in reply.

But he had hardly got going when there were three knocks at the door, which had been purposely closed, as is the custom, for Black Rod to have something to knock on, and that gentleman appeared in order to summon the Members of the House of Commons to the Lords.

When we arrived at the House of Lords it was to find more of their lordships there than usual. We did not flatter ourselves that they had assembled there to welcome us. They were there to debate the problem of Rhodesia and were waiting for the Royal Commission to be over in order to begin. As the three noble lords who were on duty on the woolsack, sitting in their red robes like so many puppets in a waxworks, took off their cocked hats with a flourish when their names were mentioned, one understood why Churchill had once described them as a Punch and Judy show.

A clerk took his place standing at the table and read out a long medieval prologue before naming the Bills which Her Majesty had agreed. At the mention of each of them another clerk intoned 'La Reine le veult'. Had La Reine looked at one of them? Nobody dreamt that she had. Neither at the Rural Water Supplies and Sewage Bill, or the Coal Industry Bill or at the Glasgow Corporation (No. 2) Confirmation Bill or at any of the others. When we filed out we knew we had been wasting the time of the lords who were waiting to speak on the Rhodesia Bill, and the way they had glared at us during the performance had convinced us that we were unwelcome guests and that they breathed a sigh of relief when they saw the backs of us.

All that actually happened was not recorded in the House of Lords *Hansard* but will duly be found in the *House of Lords Journal*.

We listened patiently to the following (extract from Journal):

The Lord Chancellor said,
'My Lords, and Members of the House of Commons,
'Her Majesty, not thinking fit to be personally present here at this time has been pleased to cause a Commission to be issued under the Great Seal, and thereby given Her Royal Assent to divers Acts which have been agreed upon by both Houses of Parliament, the titles whereof are particularly mentioned; and by the said Commission has commanded us to declare and notify Her Royal Assent to the said several Acts in the presence of you the Lords and Commons assembled for that purpose: Which Commission you will now hear read.'
Then the said Commission was read by the Clerk as follows:
'ELIZABETH R.
'Elizabeth the Second by the grace of God of the United Kingdom of Great Britain and Northern Ireland and of Our other Realms and Territories Queen, Head of the Commonwealth, Defender of the Faith; To Our right trusty and right well-beloved the Lords Spiritual and Temporal, and to Our trusty and well-beloved the knights, citizens and burgesses of the House of Commons, in this present Parliament assembled, greeting: Forasmuch as in Our said Parliament divers Acts have been agreed upon by you Our loving subjects the Lords Spiritual and Temporal, and the Commons, the short titles

of which are set forth in the schedule hereto; but the said Acts are not of force and effect in the law without Our Royal Assent; And foreasmuch as We cannot at this time be present in the Higher House of Our said Parliament, being the accustomed place for giving Our Royal Assent to such Acts as have been agreed upon by your Our said subjects, the Lords and Commons, We have therefore caused these Our Letters Patent to be made, and have signed them, and by them do give Our Royal Assent to the said Acts; Willing that the said Acts shall be of the same strength, force and effect as if We had been personally present in the said Higher House, and had publicly and in the presence of you all assented to the same: Commanding also Our well-beloved and faithful Counsellor Edward Gardner, Chancellor of Great Britain, to seal these Our Letters Patent with Our Great Seal of Our Realm; and also Commanding [here he named the three lords who sat on the bench] to declare this Our Royal Assent in the said Higher House, in the presence of you the said Lords and Commons; and the Clerk of Our Parliaments to endorse the said Acts, in Our name, as is requisite; and to enrol these Our Letters Patent, and the said Acts in manner accustomed; And finally We do declare that after this Our Royal Assent given and declared as is aforesaid, then and immediately the said Acts shall be taken and accepted as good and perfect Acts of Parliament, and be put in due execution accordingly.

'In witness whereof We have caused these Our Letters to be made patent.

Witness Ourself at Westminster, the 22nd day of December in the thirteenth year of Our reign.

'By the Queen herself, signed with Her own Hand,

'COLDSTREAM.'

Then the Lord Chancellor said,

'In obedience to Her Majesty's commands, and by virtue of the Commission which has been now read, we do declare and notify to you, the Lords Spiritual and Temporal, and Commons, in Parliament assembled, that Her Majesty hath given Her Royal Assent to the several Acts in the schedule to the Commission mentioned; and the Clerks are required to pass the same in the usual form and words.'

Then the Clerk of the House at the Table read the titles of the Bills to be passed. To these Bills the Royal Assent was pronounced as follows and as each Bill was mentioned the Clerk of Parliaments said 'La Reyne le veult':

'Expiring Laws continuance.'
'La Reyne le veult.'
'Pensions (Increase).'
'La Reyne le veult.'

'Workmens Compensation and Benefit (Amendment).'
'La Reyne le veult.'
'Rural Water Supplies and Sewage.'
'La Reyne le veult.'
'Housing (Slum Clearance Compensation).'
'La Reyne le veult.'
'Coal Industry.'
'La Reyne le veult.'
'Teachers' Superannuation.'
'La Reyne le veult.'
'Corporation of the Trinity House of Leith Order Confirmation.'
'La Reyne le veult.'
'Clyde Navigation (Superannuation Order Confirmation).'
'La Reyne le veult.'
'Clyde Port Authority Order Confirmation.'
'La Reyne le veult.'
'Glasgow Corporation (Nor) Order Confirmation.'
'La Reyne le veult.'
'Heriot-Watt College Order Confirmation.'
'La Reyne le veult.'
'Prayer Book (Versions of the Bible) Measure.'
'La Reyne le veult.'

Rather a mixed bag but the Queen had wholeheartedly approved of every one of them. All of them, including the Coal Bill, the Rural Waters and Sewage Bill, and the Prayer Book (Versions of the Bible) Measure and all the others had got safely home.

When we returned to the Chamber we found that the Member for Putney had been delivering the speech that he had prepared about the BBC and the suggested censoring of television programmes in our absence, though no Speaker had been in the chair and no Official Report had been taken of it. We knew about it because when the Postmaster-General resumed his half-delivered and half-ruined speech he announced that he would deal with the points from Putney as though his speech had been made in the debate. But though Putney had won on points there was no report in Hansard next day as to what he had said.

It certainly justified what Geoffrey de Freitas had said in an article he had written in the previous month's *New Christian* under the heading 'Parliament Choked by Tradition'.

'All of us are anxious that this country should be regarded abroad as the country it is—a modern go-ahead industrial country. I have spent many weeks this year on the Continent and in the USA and I have given a total of several hours of radio and television interviews. The questions put to me show we are regarded as a decent fuddy duddy country of beefeaters and maypoles and ceremonies. Most of us who live here are not deceived about ourselves. A people who invented radar and the jet engine must think of more than may-poles! We can see the beefeaters in perspective. But many foreigners cannot and we appear ludicrously obsessed with ceremonial. And it is not only foreigners who are critical. Many of my constituents deplore what they regard as a waste of parliamentary time on trivia.

Take our periodical pilgrimage to the Lords to hear a clerk read out the titles of Bills which have become law. How ridiculous! We break into our proceedings to parade to the Lords. Not only does it often spoil a good debate but it gives a false impression of the impor-tance of a hereditary and nominated assembly. To go once a year to the Lords when the Monarch opens Parliament is part of our history: we do not want the Monarch to come to us after our experiences 300 years ago. If it is necessary for us to be told what Bills have become law it should be done by Black Rod bringing us between Prayers and Questions a list of titles of the Acts on a silver tray.'

Sir Geoffrey de Freitas's suggestion is certainly worth con-sideration. It would save time and tempers at both ends. But why is it necessary for Black Rod to appear on the scene to carry messages on a silver tray when the whole transaction could be more promptly and efficiently carried out by Her Majesty's Post Office? One feels sure that the Postmaster-General would be delighted to arrange it.

Dr King gave his own example of mumbo-jumbo. He said:

'There was an occasion in this Parliament when one of the Cabinet Ministers—and only a Cabinet Minister can signify the Queen's Recommendation—sat for four hours through a debate in which he was not interested merely to nod his head when Mr Speaker said "Queen's Recommendation".'

He pointed out that Mr Lidderdale, the Clerk Assistant, had made the excellent suggestion that the Queen's Recommenda-tion could be signified by any Member of the Government Front Bench. There are many other suggestions that could be made to reduce the mumbo-jumbo in the place.

Even the 'Conservative' Labour Leader of the House admitted, it seemed rather grudgingly, that 'there are cobwebs to be brushed away'. From him that was a considerable concession. He would agree to the removal of the cobwebs but when it came to shifting around or removing some of the Queen Anne or Queen Victorian furniture—that was a different matter.

One thing that would help to reduce mumbo-jumbo and to remove the cobwebs from Parliament would be the introduction of television. The fact that this has been so long delayed shows how strong the resistance in Parliament is to change of any kind.

As I write the question is still under consideration, as it has been now for many years. Surely this cannot be delayed for long now. Television has become the means of mass communication and now four out of five families get their information about what is happening in this way. The interviewers on television have far better opportunities for putting searching questions to the Prime Minister or any other Cabinet Ministers and politicians than has the House of Commons. Television has now had considerable experience in the reporting of the Party Conferences and of General Election and by-election speeches and campaigns and I know of no sound reason why the House of Commons should ban it, though I can understand why the House of Lords shouldn't. The BBC's quarter of an hour nightly feature programme is an excellent piece of parliamentary reporting and there can be no objection, except perhaps from absent M.P.s, if there were a nightly television feature of the same kind. After all, the people in the county have a right to have a look at what is going on in Westminster, for they pay for it. Television could of course either kill or cure Parliament. I doubt if the viewers would want too much of it. But it might help in ending a lot of the mumbo-jumbo there.

Mr Robin Day, the television interviewer, expressed this opinion in an article in *Parliamentary Affairs* (1963) in which he wrote 'Television would stimulate the House of Commons to modernize its procedure and improve the standard of debate' and argues that if the antiquated proceedings of Parliament were exposed on the screen public opinion would be aroused for parliamentary reform.

This is a refreshingly candid outside view, although Allan Segan in an appendix to Professor Bernard Crick's view thinks that it is putting the cart before the horse with a vengeance.

On this I am all on the side of Robin Day. If television has to wait until parliamentary reform changes things in the House of Commons it may have to wait for another ten years (Dr King's estimate) or twenty years (Mr Bowden's). It will have to wait a very long time, by which time television will be reporting everything except Parliament. Many of the objections made to the televising of the House have also been made to the televising of church services. Now many of the churches are concerned not with how to keep television out of their services but how to get it in.

The memorial service to Richard Dimbleby in Westminster Abbey was televised in a way that Richard Dimbleby would have heartily approved. Television has come and Parliament, like every other national institution, must be prepared to take the risks.

If Mr Turton's point is a good one, and I certainly think it is, that its proceedings should be intelligible to people outside, M.P.s must learn to speak using less parliamentary jumbo if they are to be understood by a TV audience. After all, M.P.s are used to seeing their speeches edited or summarized or more often omitted altogether in the popular Press. There are recent indications that Parliament is prepared to reconsider its repeated refusals to have television in, although on one occasion the Queen's Opening of Parliament was televised and no serious objection was taken to it. But there is no reason why the experiment should not be tried. It could always be abandoned if it were considered that the difficulties were insuperable or if there was reason to believe that the viewing public found it too boring and switched it off.

Exactly how and in what form the proceedings of Parliament should be televised is a question of trial and error. One never knows what it would be like until it is tried.

Aneurin Bevan was one of those who strongly advocated the television of Parliament. Speaking in the debate on the Address in 1959 he said:

'At the beginning of this Parliament I am going to suggest that a serious investigation takes place into the technical possibilities of televising parliamentary proceedings.'

Mr Cyril Osborne (Louth): 'Oh, no, Nye.'

Mr Bevan: 'I know that Members shake their heads, but why should they be so shy? . . . All I am suggesting is that in these days when all the apparatus of mass suggestion are against demo-cratic education, we should seriously consider re-establishing intelli-gent communication between the House of Commons and the elec-torate as a whole. That is surely a democratic process.'

In his little pamphlet *The Case for Televising Parliament* (Hansard Society), Robin Day says that Bevan had tackled him vigorously about the problems of televising Parliament and he had quickly grasped the essential point that Parliament should not be shut off from the power of television. So Robin Day was less surprised than others when this suggestion was made from the despatch box. What particularly disturbed Bevan was the system under which politicians were granted access to tele-vision's powerful platform. This was one of the main reasons he gave for televising Parliament.

'Recently, and not only recently but for many years now, there has grown up what I consider a most humiliating state of affairs in which Members of this House are picked out to take part in tele-vision broadcasts at the *ipse dixit* of the bureaucracy at Broadcasting House. In fact there has been nothing so humiliating than to see Members of Parliament in responsible positions selected by unrepre-sentative persons to have an opportunity of appearing on the radio or television . . . Also what is almost worse, political alternatives are not placed before the people in a realistic fashion because of the selection of speakers that takes place. I have complained about this on many occasions.'

Bevan followed this up by a demand which staggered the most enthusiastic supporters of televising Parliament. He said:

'There ought to be a special channel that they can turn on and listen to us at any time. I am not arguing that we should have only special debates televised, but there should be a special channel for the House of Commons itself.'

It was not difficult to dispose of this idea. Most of a day's proceedings in Parliament would be deadly dull for any outside person unfamiliar with the routine of the House of Commons. They could, if they wished, pick and choose between the times that were likely to interest them. But they would soon get tired of switching on and off for the spicy items, and nobody quite

M

knows in Parliament when they are likely to come on, that the proposed channel would soon be permanently switched off.

Mr Robin Day's suggestion of an edited half-hour at the end of the day was far better. The television authorities would soon discover what interested the public and what didn't.

It would be wise to let the TV specialists have a go. A good many things would have to be decided by experiment, by trial and error, and the really interesting items could be featured again next day.

The points made by Robin Day are sound. This method:

1. Would not monopolize a special channel.
2. It would enable Question Time and important afternoon speeches to be seen in the evening by much bigger audiences.
3. There would be no problem as to which M.P.s are called at peak viewing hours. All would have a reasonable chance of inclusion in a late-evening edited report.
4. Tedious procedural matters could be omitted, thus avoiding the fear (exposed by Mr Gaitskell) that hours of infinite boredom would be inflicted on the public.

I could add many more reasons for bringing television in. It might help to cut down verbosity. M.P.s might learn to say in ten minutes what now takes them half an hour, thus giving a chance for more speakers and more points of view. If the way we have in the House of Commons of referring to each other as 'honourable Members', 'honourable and gallant Members' and 'Right honourable and learned Members' has become old fashioned and archaic, why not drop it?

When Mr Quintin Hogg arrived back in the House of Commons he had to be referred to as 'the Right honourable and learned Member for Marylebone' and at first we asked our neighbours 'Who's he?' and the answer was 'Hogg'. Everybody knew who 'Hogg' was. This is just one example of how we can waste time. Hogg is one syllable. To refer to him in Parliament takes sixteen. I know one Scots Member who cannot refer to other members in the House without saying honourable Members, honourable and gallant Members, honourable and learned members, right honourable . . . , etc., etc., and as this occurred more than once in a speech it was half an hour's unmitigated anguish for the M.P. who was waiting to follow him. The best explanation I could offer for this was that he enjoyed every syllable because he imagined that it was a sip of whisky. Of course ITV would never stand for this, it would upset the advertising.

Dickens laughed at the Circumlocution Office. He knew. He had been a reporter in the gallery. We used to know when Sir Alec Douglas Home was Prime Minister who M.P.s were talking about. When somebody now refers to the honourable Member for Kinross and West Perthshire, one wonders whether he means one of the Liberal Members for the Highlands until somebody from behind translates it into *Hume*. There are of course exceptions. It is easier to refer to the honourable Member for Salisbury than to Sir Hugh Munro-Lucas-Tooth.

If in the TV debates the honourable and learned Member for Marylebone had always to refer to the Right honourable Member for Easington some one would promptly say 'Chuck it boys, we've only a quarter of an hour'. The TV editors would soon learn to cut out the circumlocution jargon and the points of order that the outside audience wouldn't appreciate or understand. This would mean a lot of work for them for translation of the House of Commons English into ordinary English would take time. One explanation of this way of M.P.s referring to one another was that it was dangerous for M.P.s to be named because it would mean trouble for them outside.

But anonymity is not what M.P.s exactly want these days. The time has undoubtedly come for the House to consider whether it is not time to abandon many of its ancient habits. Why should a very mediocre barrister need always to be called 'the honourable and learned Member' while a capable solicitor who probably knows a great deal more about the law than he does be just 'honourable'? Indeed, why should the legal profession be referred to as if they were the only 'learned' people in the House. What about the university dons and lecturers, the schoolmasters, the doctors, the research chemists and all the other professional people? Why should we perpetuate the snobbery of the law courts in the House of Commons?

Then why should an ex-officer be the only person to be called 'gallant', even if he has seen less of war than an ex-private opposite. The military snobbery is as out-of-date as the legal snobbery. Any of the M.P.s who have worked in the coal mines have seen more real danger than the soldiers or the naval commanders, or the group captains in the R.A.F. There ought to be no distinctions of this kind in a democratic Parliament. They are survivals of the past, like the fast disappearing tile hats on Budget Day and the snuff box at the entrance of the House.

And what a ridiculous spectacle is presented when a Member wishes to raise a point of order and can only do it when he is 'seated and covered' and a tile hat kept in reserve by the Sergeant at Arms is hurriedly produced and passed quickly from one Member to another like a rugby football. Usually the tile doesn't fit and the M.P., who may have quite a serious point of order to raise, is made to look plain silly.

One objection of M.P.s is that TV would act as a terribly efficient detective. It would reveal what M.P.s were there and who were not and would lead to misunderstanding. The TV might become an awful Big Brother that one would always have to think about, whether one was in Westminster or out of it.

So the TV could take a look occasionally at the committees, and the library, and the M.P.s writing at their desks, which would reveal that they were on the job. Indeed the TV could do no harm if it showed the public that M.P.s were as human as anybody else and needed time to relax. That does not mean that they should necessarily intrude into the bar without due warning, knowing that the unfortunate incident of the Lord Chancellor photographed upsetting his sherry has led to the burning of photographs on the terrace (except by special licence) for so many years.

Mr Herbert Bowden, the Leader of the House under Mr Wilson's Government, however, has attacked the idea of televising the House as 'frightening'.

'I do not like the idea . . . I do not want Parliament to become an alternative to "That Was the Week That Was".'

But if the burlesque of Parliament is going to be the only idea of it that is conveyed to the general public this is unfair to Parliament. It is true that Parliament has its moments of the grotesque, but so have the party conferences. So have the law courts. Why should we be 'frightened' if we have nothing to hide?

Mr Bowden put the stock parliamentary objections to televising the House when he said:

'Through you, Mr Speaker, we address each other in debate. We
are not speaking to the country or to the world outside. It is true
that reports of our debates appear in *Hansard*. But the very intimacy
of our debates would be lost if the atmosphere were not as it is. . . .
I am very much afraid that once the television cameras swing into
action the whole atmosphere of this Chamber would change . . . I
have noticed that this House has its moods. It has its hilarious
moods, its serious moods, and very often when an important statement is imminent we are often apprehensive and giggle like schoolgirls. I think that is right. It is right that Members of Parliament
should react in that way. If an important statement is expected, the
apprehensions about what its effects may be in the country have
their effects upon us. A great deal of that would be lost if it were
felt that the television cameras were trained on us. Television would
add nothing to our proceedings or our dignity.'

Mr Harold Macmillan said later 'I am bound to say, if I give
my personal opinion, that that was exactly the argument which
was presented against the publication of *Hansard*'.

M.P.s would soon get used to television just as the delegates
to the party conferences have. It has not done them any harm
and their discussions are as serious as any of the debates in
Parliament. The House of Commons can be too obsessed with
its privileges and its dignity.

As a Scots Member I see no reason why the Scottish Grand
Committee in session should not be televised occasionally or a
pilot experiment not tried out there. Certainly it would give a
better impression as a businesslike, more efficient body, operating in the twentieth century, than the proceedings in the
Chamber downstairs. We are, in a way, a miniature Parliament
of our own. Here ancient rituals are dispensed with and we get
to work quickly with two taps of the Chairman's mallet and
the words 'Order, Order'. The debating is as good as downstairs
and the speeches are usually shorter and there is less rhetoric.
The authority of the chair is just as much respected although
the Chairman does not wear a wig and neither do the clerks,
and nobody misses the mace.

This is what any deliberative assembly should be like in these
days. Scots M.P.s would get on with the work that has to be
done, whether the TV were there or not, and they have no need

to fear if their constituents had a look at what was on. Indeed it would be a considerable help if the people of Scotland were familiarized with the problems which face the Government in Scotland and what steps are being taken to deal with them.

CHAPTER 21

THE MINISTERIAL ESTABLISHMENT

The Labour Government that was elected by a tiny majority in October 1964 in the middle of an economic crisis and with all kinds of problems bequeathed to it by thirteen years of Conservative rule could not be expected to undertake a considerable measure of parliamentary reform. One cannot see any government, except a progressively-minded government with a good working majority and a determined Parliament, attempting this.

But the Government might have accepted the recommendations of the Committee on Procedure on Select Committee which had been carried with only two dissentients at the committee and which had Liberal and also Conservative support.

Here the Government, whose views were expressed by the Leader of the House, showed unnecessary timidity and a reluctance to agree to what were only after all cautious and moderate proposals for change.

The Times and even the Daily Telegraph, in a leading article 'Can One Know Too Much?', had approved of them.

'The Committee on Procedure has gone a long way towards making the proposals of the Study of Parliament Group their own. Their approach is more gradual and the task they would give these specialist committees more circumscribed. But unlike their predecessors, they accept the need for some such advice and believe it can be made to work without the attendant evils of which so much is made in English analyses of foreign legislature.

'Total opposition to the idea came from Mr Enoch Powell, a witness, and Mr Michael Foot, a member of the committee. The minutes of evidence contain the Powellian paradox "I think it a common fallacy to suppose Members are any more effective in criticizing an administration because they are well informed . . . the more information Members have the less effective they are likely to be in debate and the more likely to approximate to the point of view of the Minister and his department".

'Mr Foot sees the proposal as an obstacle to the true objective of reform which should be to "restore the authority of the House of

Commons Chamber itself" and as "likely to nurture the miserable deception that more and more can gradually be taken out of politics".

'There is truth in these robust dissents but their truth does not really conflict with what is proposed. It is to attribute excessive feeble-mindedness in M.P.s to assume that because they are put in possession of the full departmental brief, as it were, they will therefore slip into acquiescence in ministerial policy. Nor is it clear why spadework done "in committee upstairs" need detract from the importance of debates in the Chamber when it could well make those debates authoritative. As for the fear that political conflict might be dimmed because Parliament informs itself more fully about the activities of government the fear implies that the conflict only thrives in conditions of ignorance. If that were so, which it is not, there would be no reason to regret the abatement of political conflict." '

When a reform is supported in *The Times* even in the most cautious language one can depend upon it that such a reform is long overdue.

The leading article in the *Daily Telegraph* said:

'It is natural that Ministers and potential Ministers generally look askance at any proposal to develop the watching powers of the Commons. It is amusing to see that old rebel Mr Michael Foot joining Sir Martin Redmayne in what appears to be the views of the Ministerial Establishment. Mr Foot argues that these proposals are a diversion from the main issue which is to restore the authority of the House of Commons Chamber itself. Yet that is precisely the committee's aim. The weakness of debates on the Estimates is that they tend to be ill informed. The increased flexibility and spontaneity which Mr Foot rightly demands are only a part of the answer. He is correct to give a warning against committee proliferation as a parliamentary disease but he should not urge his objections against those committees concerned with the fundamentals of Parliamentary power. How to reassert the power of the Commons both to defend the liberty of the subject and to prevent the misuse of public funds in a period of expanding bureaucracy is one of the great problems of this age. The Committee on Procedure is right in its belief that a solution is possible which achieves these aims and yet avoids, as it were, interference with the administrative work from day to day.'

The editor of the *Daily Telegraph*, in referring to the Ministerial Establishment, struck the nail on the head. This is the real and potential danger to any move to change parliamentary procedure that may be a threat to its power and position.

This is what Mr Bowden expressed when in his concluding

speech in the debate of December 1965 he said 'In paragraph 8 of the Report we are told that it is not wished that the Select Committee should get involved in party politics but how can we avoid it once we get into the realms of policy? In paragraph 9 we are told that the committee agrees that it is not easy to differentiate between pure policy questions and other questions, so we are back again to square one and the difficulty of decision in this field.'

Of course if we were never to appoint a parliamentary committee in case it would get involved in party policy we would never have any committees at all nor indeed any democracy. The Leader of the House would solve this problem by washing his hands of the idea of specialist committees and leaving the present procedure as it is.

There is something ironic about party politicians getting upset about the need for avoiding party politics as if it were something particularly filthy. Surely that is what Parliament is about. Indeed one of the duties of Parliament is to keep a watchful eye on establishments, especially ministerial ones. Would the Committee of Estimates or the Committee of Public Accounts ever be able to report on anything if they had not been prepared to risk stepping on some ministerial toes?

Now if a Minister is scared of having a committee interested in his department it must be because he has something to hide, something he or his civil servants do not want Parliament to know about it.

Mr L. Amery, speaking from his own experience of office, expressed the view that such committees would have been helpful to him as a Minister. A Minister could be helped if he could relegate some of the matters he has to decide upon for consideration of a committee on which were members who might have considerable experience to draw upon. There might be aspects of some problem about which civil servants have little knowledge. In the House of Commons there is a great deal of experience in many spheres which would be called on. Is that not what Members are there for? Many Ministers would have been spared awkward moments in Parliament if some matter had been scrutinized in a committee before an unexpected storm had blown up in the House.

Why should a Labour Government be scared at the very

mention of specialist committees as the Leader of the House appeared to be? Labour Members, administrators, trade unionists have all grown up in the atmosphere of committees. The Labour Party and the T.U.C. and the Co-operative Movement has them. In fact it would be impossible for any democratic movement to function at all if it created a class of officials who resented committees. There are in the Civil Service men in positions of power who would no doubt like to be a law unto themselves and so also would some Ministers. Why should a democratic Labour Party acquiesce in a Ministerial Establishment when it has come into existence to challenge so many other establishments. Parliament is entitled to defend itself against the possibility of a strong bureaucrat and a weak Minister, against a Minister who uncritically reads out official briefs without understanding them.

As Professor Bernard Crick put it :

'A committee controlled by party settlement can be a sounding board and a testing ground for ministerial projects, and it could be a valuable help to a Minister in his own problems—in itself almost as great as those we have been discussing—of keeping control of his own department. Many of the present party committees have amicable and mutually helpful relationships with Ministers.'

There is another danger to a Labour Government in a Ministerial Establishment. It could result in the Parliamentary Labour Party being divided into Ministers and non-Ministers, and this division could appear in the party in the country.

One has to remember too that the Ministerial Establishment is not just confined to one side of the House. On the other side is the preventive Ministerial Establishment. This has developed considerably in recent years. Now we have the Shadow Cabinet with Shadow Ministers of all kinds watching the Ministers whose jobs they hope to get after the next General Election. They may think that they would prefer not to have these committees either. The result could very well develop into a Ministers' and Prospective Ministers' Establishment which could easily become a conspiracy against the non-ministerial House, a conspiracy of Front Benchers v. Back Benchers. The House of Commons always needs to be watchful when they find Government and Opposition spokesmen billing and cooing at each other across the table confirming some agreement they have reached behind the Speaker's chair and looking grieved and pained when some back bencher wants to know what it is all about.

Again there is Mr Turton's point about the people in the gallery and those outside. If they are entitled to have a procedure that is intelligible are they not entitled to have the fullest information on the subject that the House of Commons is debating about?

A committee's report which contains evidence in question and answer form is often the most readable document that comes from Her Majesty's Stationery Office. One learns quicker from that than from a mass of figures served up as indigestible statistics and tables, or from a long, dreary exposition that may come from a Minister reading a brief. These are the days when television has stimulated a great public interest in what is happening day by day in the country and throughout the world. If we want an intelligent and well-informed electorate we should give them the maximum amount of information we can about the many problems that M.P.s are faced with today. A Labour Government has everything to gain if the electorate know as much as can be known about everything under the sun. The Press and the radio and the TV should be able to pass on to the public what the debates on the big issues are about. 'Let the people know' should be the motto of a government that seeks to rally people behind it to co-operate with it in building up the new society. Government should not be regarded as an establishment, or as a secret society. The people are entitled to know what is being done and what needs to be done in order that they can play their part.

CHAPTER 22

WHY GENERAL ELECTIONS?

When the result of the General Election of 1964 became known, with Labour in with a small majority, we were told that it just meant another General Election in a short time although that might mean that another General Election might bring very much the same result again. People had cast their votes for their M.P.s to send them to the House of Commons to represent them for five years. Nobody said 'Well this is what the people of Britain have decided, go in and make the best of it for another five years and don't bother us again until the five years are up.'

But under our present Constitution the Prime Minister is given the power to call for an election perhaps in a year or maybe two years' time, because he thinks it the appropriate time for his party to go to the poll on the chance that it will come back again.

In a municipal election you elect a member for three years and the chairman has no right to dissolve the town council or the county council during that time. And our councils are not less sensibly run than Parliament. If a proposal for a new slaughter house is defeated the chairman has no right to regard this as a vote of no-confidence and for all the councillors to come out and stand an election again.

The situation that arose as a result of the General Election of 1964 should certainly have made many people think whether our present arrangements are sensible ones. Under our present law fixing the duration of Parliament for a maximum period of five years Sir Alec Douglas-Home was compelled to come to the country in October. The previous Tory Governments had not lasted that time because they thought they could get their majority if they came to the country earlier. Their strategy was based on a policy of producing a budget which gave an entirely false picture of the economic prosperity of the country—'You've never had it so good', etc.—and which enabled them to trick the country into believing that the Tories had made a good job of government. Then when the elections were over the inevitable financial crisis came and another Budget was necessary to deal with it. But having got back into power the Tories were able to give more concessions to the wealthy vested interests that had supported them and paid for the Tory Party organization and filled their election coffers and paid the bills for the mass advertising campaigns that went on for the year preceding the election.

Had misfortune not overtaken Mr Macmillan he would probably have attempted the same thing again. His successor, Sir Alec Douglas Home, on being appointed Prime Minister, immediately went to a Conservative meeting to say that the main preoccupation must be the coming General Election. But he was advised by his party organizers that the Tories would lose if an election took place in the Spring of 1964 and so it was delayed until October when it would have had to take place anyway. A year before this Mr Macmillan had said that the uncertainty over an election was one of the factors that led to lack of confidence and increased unemployment. That however did not evidently count with Sir Alec.

Mr Maudling was reported to have been in favour of a Spring election. If that were so it would have been understandable because as Chancellor of the Exchequer he must have known that another financial crisis was on the horizon and had the Tories won he would have had to handle it, probably in very much the same way and introducing some of the same measures for which the Tories in Opposition bitterly attacked his successor.

The result was that the Labour Government had to find the money for the bills that the Tories had not paid, found it had to deal with the financial crisis that had been bequeathed to it and had to face an immediate wave of unpopularity. Indeed had an election taken place, as a result of a few Labour M.P.s dying as a result of some accident in the Spring of 1965, a subsequent General Election might have resulted in big Tory gains and a Tory Government established again in power for another five years.

Has not the time come then for the consideration of fixed elections without the Prime Minister of the day having the power to call for a dissolution of Parliament?

Five years has been hitherto decided as a reasonable record for election of M.P.s. But is there any reason why they should be all elected at a General Election at the same time. Why should not a fifth of them stand for election every year? In the municipalities a third of the councillors retire each year. Why should not a fifth of the M.P.s retire every year? Each constituency would then know exactly when it would vote for a Member. Let me illustrate how it would work out in the county of Ayrshire, which I know best. Here there are five constituencies—Ayr, Kilmarnock, Central Ayrshire, North Ayrshire and South Ayrshire. The M.P. for each would have to stand for re-election every five years. In the county, however, there would be one parliamentary election every year. Interest in politics would therefore not flare up every four or five years during which time it would be maintained for all the political issues of the day as the election in the one constituency took place. If we are to have an educated electorate interest in politics should not be sporadic but continuous. Party workers and organizers from all the surrounding constituencies would come in and so would the national speakers and the radio commentators and TV cameras. The electors would have a far better opportunity to know exactly what the election was about and candidates would not be so lost and isolated as they are in General Elections where all the country is polling on the same day.

Now this is such a radical departure from our usual idea of parliamentary elections that it is bound to meet with opposition from those who object to new political ideas of any kind and are content to vote as their grandfathers and great grandfathers voted before them, even if they had no right to vote at all.

The Conservatives would of course flatly turn the idea down. They would argue that this would give an immense advantage to the Labour Party because it would concentrate their party workers from all around on a constituency on polling day. The Conservatives of course would be able to do that too. This objection could only work on the assumption that whereas the Labour Party workers are voluntary the Conservative Party depends more on a party machine whose workers are paid. The reply to that of course is that the Conservative Party is really the party of the few. If it is not, if the Conservative Party is composed of a vast army of voluntary enthusiasts who can also come in, then they have nothing to be alarmed about. On the other hand the Conservatives have advantages over the Labour Party because the Press is preponderatingly on their side. So are the powerful landlord interests in the rural areas where there are still voters who have their doubts whether the ballot is all that secret when they see the gentry and the lairds with the big rosettes so active outside the schools on election day and where Labour voters who do think that the ballot is secret still fear to put the Labour candidates' election cards in their windows.

Then how would this method of electing affect the marginal seats. Would they still be so marginal or would they not go Labour? One never can be sure of these things but my guess is that they would. The main reason for this is that with increased political activity and discussion, with all the issues being fiercely argued about, the Labour Party has most to gain.

It would also test the propaganda of all parties. The Conservative Party would have better opportunities to explain its new programmes and the electorate better able to understand what alternatives it had to offer to those of Labour. The Liberals too should welcome this new method of election because it would give them better opportunities to explain where exactly they stood in politics. From the point of the electorate this idea would have considerable advantages. Each constituency would know when it would have to vote for a Member and who would represent it for the following five years. The fight would be, as it is now, for the marginal seats, but the floating voters would have more information about the rival parties and be better able to decide whether they were going to continue to float or sink.

It may be thought, however, that a four-year or three-year term of office (as in the local authorities) would be better. I only fix it at five years because that is now the term which a Parliament may last if a dissolution is not called for by the Prime Minister.

How would this affect a Government? The party with the majority would form a Government but it would have to carry out a policy which it knew would be approved of by the electorate. It would know that it might lose this majority in a year's time if it tried to repeat the policy of Conservative Governments between 1951 and 1964, that is introduce a Budget in which it

set out to bribe the electorate before a General Election, knowing that it would have to face a financial crisis after it had been
returned. With one-fifth of the M.P.s retiring every year 120
seats would have to be filled in a year's time and any Government would have to keep this in mind. Chancellors of the
Exchequer would be less in danger of being tempted to introduce vote-catching instead of honest budgets and less liable to
have their feelings hurt by being accused afterwards of cooking
the books. If we are in an economic mess because a Government
has not paid its bills then the taxpayer has a right to know about
it and not to be bamboozled or presented at election time with
a fraudulent prospectus.

During the parliamentary struggle over the Finance Bill of
1964 when the Labour Government was only getting its tax
proposals through by one or two votes, I often thought it would
be a good arrangement if the Opposition were to be allowed to
take over the day after it had defeated the Government and
handle the financial crisis with the same kind of majority, no
General Election being possible. Indeed a General Election under
these circumstances, and it could have happened had a few
Labour M.P.s been killed in an accident, would have been the
most colossal political swindle of recent times with the Opposition gambling on the temporary unpopularity that the Labour
Government was going through owing to having to face the
problems inherited by its predecessors. One remembers how
Labour Governments before the war were overthrown by waves
of panic caused by scares and stunts and then the long years of
Tory rule that ultimately ended in the catastrophe of World
War Two. The Macmillan tactics would have been impossible if
a year after a Tory election victory there would have been a
fifth of the M.P.s coming to face the electorate again. It is much
easier for a Chancellor of the Exchequer to cook the books than
a finance committee of a town council or a county council.
Again the Macmillan Governments had a trick of introducing
the legislation which helped its friends in the first year or two
after an election, hoping that the electorate would forget about
this when the General Election came along in four years' time.
To those who argue that this would lead to unstable government I would reply that one of the worst governments that this
country has had this century was the Government that was

elected on the slogan 'Vote for Baldwin and a stable Government!' A Government that gets a substantial majority and then says 'We are all right, boys, for four or five years and forget about the electorate until another General Election time is approaching' can be a cynical, do-little, we-can-fool-them-again-the-next-time Government, as so many have been in the past. No Government should be allowed to forget the electorate for one moment. A Government should always be kept on its toes.

What we need is more alert and more progressively-minded Governments and a better educated and better informed electorate.

I would carry the democratic process a little further. Should not the Members of a Government be elected by the House of Commons and not selected by a Prime Minister? If we really believe in democracy we ought not to give a blank negative to this question which will certainly flutter the dove cotes at Westminster.

I have pointed out earlier what enormous power is now in the hands of a Prime Minister. In a recent television debate I was told that the Prime Minister must select his team. That is the stock answer, as if the work of government is just a game of cricket or football. But at Westminster the team has become so big that the Prime Minister is in a position not only to select the team but a large number of the supporters as well. It was frequently alleged against Harold Macmillan that his team included some of his relatives who were not just chosen on their merits. Nobody was able to accuse Harold Wilson of giving jobs to his sons-in-law, for none were available. Leaving the Wilson Government out of the argument, what has happened in previous Labour Governments? When Ramsay Macdonald had to form his first Labour Government in 1924 he had to find jobs for certain leaders, not necessarily because they were the men best qualified by experience and ability for their particular jobs but because they held important positions in the party or the trade union movement. He had to think twice before ignoring this group or that. Attlee had to do the same when he had to form his Governments. This seems to a considerable extent unavoidable under the present system and it places an enormous task and responsibility on one man. Is it the best method of getting the right men in the right places? In balancing the claims to

N

office of one man or group against another, is the final result the right men in the right places?

Nobody can say confidently unless the alternative method is tried—that is election as against selection. Ought not a trial be given to the democratic system? It might not work, but ought it not to be tried? The Labour, trade union and Co-operative movements are based upon the principle of election. The Labour Party chooses its Executive by election, the Leader does not choose the members. The President of the T.U.C. does not choose the General Council either. Nor does the Chairman of the Co-operative movement choose his fellow directors. In the business world the directors of big companies, in theory at least, are elected by their shareholders. Bishops of course are selected but not elected, but when we appoint a Government we are not choosing a collection of bishops.

In the House of Commons the Speaker is elected. The House of Lords is not considered fit to elect its own Speaker, the Lord Chancellor, he is chosen for it.

We elect the Deputy Speaker, the Chairman of Committees and his deputy.

What then is wrong to consider whether Cabinet Ministers should not be elected by the Members? Working together on committees gives Members an opportunity of judging the calibre and competence and experience of other Members on the subjects with which they are dealing. These qualities should count more than a Prime Minister's political necessities of appointing people because of their place in the political world. This not only applies to Government but to Opposition. The practice in recent years of giving the Leader power to appoint a very large number of M.P.s into shadow posts in a Shadow Government gives him very great power to reward his friends and to conciliate and neutralize his critics and potential enemies in a party. There have been instances of this in both parties. In his day as Leader, Mr Gaitskell capriciously removed Mr Crossman from his shadow post of spokesman on pensions because he had differed with him on defence policy. Mr Gaitskell's Shadow Cabinet was overburdened with Right Wing personalities because they were, or were assumed to be, followers of the 'Gaitskell line'. One does not quite know the reasons why Mr Heath sent Mr Henry Brooke or Mr Julian Amery to the back benches. Men of experience and ability can be dispensed with by a party leader to make way for somebody who has less of these qualities but has a capacity for intrigue and subservience.

The capacity to jump from one band wagon to another by the pushing and ambitious politicians mainly concerned with advancing their own claims to promotion is no unusual phenomenon at Westminster. But it does not follow that the persons most adept at this necessarily make the better Ministers or administrators. Nobody with a knowledge of human nature can have any delusion that election of Ministers would solve these problems or perhaps not bring new ones, but the present system undoubtedly gives too much power to leaders of parties and does not always bring the best results.

That is why I favour the election method instead of the selection one for the Cabinet and for the main positions in the Government. Once a committee system was fully established the committees might appoint the junior ministers themselves either as chairmen or deputy chairmen of the committees. The more experienced members of the committees who knew the talent available would have a better knowledge of the best person for the job than a Prime Minister or the whips.

This is all part of the greater democratization of Parliament than exists at present. If the objection is made that this has never been done before the answer obviously is that if we are to modernize Parliament many things will have to be done for which there is no precedent and if it is said that these ideas are unworkable it is an easy enough matter to get some hints of how it can be done from the building that runs the government of London on the other side of the river.

To anyone who replies that we do not want to see the House of Commons become a glorified county council I would say that we have a lot to learn from county councils who have not the hoary old traditions and customs tied around their necks, and as they did not exist in their present forms either in the reign of King William or Queen Anne, to say nothing of those which go further back still, are more in line with the times and more democratic in every way. Are we really in a position at Westminster to pose as ever so superior persons to the members of the county councils who may have far greater knowledge and experience of the problems with which the people they represent

are faced with than we have. We have no right to regard ourselves as more efficient public servants (many M.P.s would
probably feel horrified and insulted at this description) than the
town councillors or indeed the parish councillors. Nor should we
be disdainful of the parish pump. It may not be so antiquated
as a lot we see daily at Westminster at which an octogenarian
parish councillor on a remote parish council in the wilds of
Inverness-shire would laugh.

I do not see how Parliament can go on in the old ways and
still have the respect of a newer generation which is always
being exhorted to pull its weight so that Britain can survive in
a modern world which is changing so quickly. We are being
repeatedly told that we have to modernize our railways, our
shipyards, our coal mines and factories, our agriculture and our
education, and we have appointed a Minister of Technology to
advise us on how it can be done.

When a wage claim is made from any section of industry
Mr George Brown promptly refers it to the Incomes and Prices
Committee and the answer often promptly comes that by
adopting modern productivity methods we can increase the
efficiency of an industry in other ways.

Indeed we are hearing that the time has come for a complete
reorganisation of local government in order to make it more
rational and modern. I have always thought that it was a bit of
effrontery on the part of the people in or behind the Government to talk like this as long as in our Government at Westminster our motto is 'No Change'.

The Speaker in a recent television interview expressed an
opinion to the effect that the new Members from both parties
who arrived after the 1964 General Election were of a better
quality than he had ever known before. I think he was right.
The revolt of many of them against the traditional mumbo-
jumbo of Westminster is a healthy sign of the times, and so is
the new attention that the Press and public is giving to what is
going on in the House of Commons.

If we are really marching on to a new civilization the time
has come to leave mumbo-jumbo behind.

Appendix 1

Speaker's Procession

1. Each day before the House meets, the Speaker moves in procession from his residence to the Chamber.[1]

2. Five minutes before the Speaker is due to be in the Chair, the following assemble in the ante-room to the Speaker's Library:

> Sergeant at Arms
> Speaker's Secretary
> Chaplain
> Trainbearer
> Bar Doorkeeper

3. On the Speaker emerging from the Library, all bow, and the Bar Doorkeeper then places the Mace on the right shoulder of the Sergeant at Arms and the Procession moves off as follows:

> Bar Doorkeeper
> Sergeant at Arms with Mace
> Speaker, with train held by Trainbearer
> Speaker's Secretary and Chaplain, side by side,
> > the latter on the right

by way of the Library Corridor, Smoking Room Corridor, Lower Waiting Hall, Central Lobby and Members Lobby.

4. As the Procession passes the outer door of the Chamber:

(a) The Bar Doorkeeper steps to the right in the Bar Lobby, turns inwards, halts and bows to the Sergeant at Arms and the Speaker.

(b) The Sergeant at Arms proceeds well inside the inner door of the Chamber and moves slightly to the right, awaiting the arrival of the Speaker.

(c) The Speaker's train is placed on his left arm by the Trainbearer, who steps to the left and then proceeds via the 'Aye' Lobby to the Speaker's Lobby at the Back of the Chair.

(d) Members in the Chamber rise in their places and remove their hats.

5. On arriving at the inner door of the Chamber:

(a) The Speaker passes through, coming up on the left of the Sergeant at Arms; and side by side, they step to the Bar, where they pause and bow.

(b) The Speaker's Secretary and the Chaplain follow into the Chamber, halting and bowing when the Speaker and Sergeant at Arms bow at the Bar. The Speaker's Secretary then turns and retires to the Back of the Chair via the Bar Lobby and 'Aye' Lobby; and the Chaplain continues to follow the Speaker and Sergeant at Arms.

6. From the Bar the Speaker and Sergeant at Arms, side by side, take

---

[1] A detailed account of the trek that has to be undertaken by the Speaker before he finally arrives in the chair is to be found in the little book *Ceremonial in the House of Commons* by Lieutenant-Colonel Thorne, the Assistant Sergeant at Arms. It records every turn and every bow.

six paces which bring them between the centre gangway and the Table; here they pause and bow before advancing again : the Speaker proceeds to the left (west) side of the Table, where he awaits the Chaplain while the Sergeant at Arms places the Mace on the Table, bows and returns to his chair, bowing at the Bar. In the meantime the Chaplain has been following them to the Table, bowing at the Bar and at the centre gangway; he passes on to the right end of the Table. From their positions at the opposite sides of the Table the Speaker and Chaplain bow to the empty Chair, turn inwards, bow to each other and then take their places at the Table. The Principal Doorkeeper announces 'Speaker at Prayers' and rings the Division Bells. The Bar Doorkeepers and the Doorkeepers at the Back of the Chair close the doors of the Chamber, so that no one may enter while the Speaker is at Prayers.

7. The Chaplain begins with Psalm 67 to say the prayers and when he reaches the words 'Let us Pray' :

(a) The Speaker and Chaplain (who have been standing) kneel on stools at the Table.

(b) Members (who have been facing the floor of the House) turn towards their seats for the remainder of the prayers.

(c) The Sergeant at Arms, who has been standing in front of his chair facing the Speaker, turns round and kneels on it while prayers are being said.

8. When prayers are over the Speaker and Chaplain stand up, turn inwards and bow to each other; the Speaker takes the Chair; and the Principal Doorkeeper announces 'Prayers are over' and 'Speaker in the Chair' and rings the Division Bells.

9. The Chaplain walks backwards from the Chamber bowing at the Table, at the centre gangway and at the Bar.

10. As soon as prayers are over the Doorkeepers at the back of the Chair enter the Chamber from the Speaker's Lobby and place under the Table the stools on which the Speaker and the Chaplain have been kneeling; stow away the prayer books; and place in position the chairs for the Clerk of the House and his two Assistants.

(1) The Assistant Sergeant at Arms proceeds to the Members Lobby ten minutes before the Speaker is due in the Chair and is responsible for order being kept in the Lobby.

(2) (a) When the Procession is half-way along the Library Corridor, the Police Constable outside the Library Door calls 'Speaker' and removes his helmet.

(b) As soon as the Procession approaches the Lower Waiting Hall, the Police Constable there calls 'Speaker' and removes his helmet; in the Central Lobby the Inspector of Police orders 'Hats off, Strangers'. The Police remove their head-dress and the public and any Members present remove their hats. The Inspector of Police is responsible for the order being obeyed.

(3) On the call 'Speaker' being heard in the Members Lobby :

(a) The Assistant Sergeant at Arms places himself alongside the

Second Principal Doorkeeper's chair;

(b) The Doorkeepers form up, in two lines facing inwards between the Commons Corridor and the door of the House.

(4) As the Procession approaches the Members Lobby, the Principal Doorkeeper proceeds to the Bar, bows and announces 'Speaker'; then he returns to the Bar Lobby, where he stands while the Procession moves into the Chamber. As the Sergeant at Arms and the Speaker pass, two bows are made by the Assistant Sergeant at Arms and Doorkeepers.

(5) The announcement 'Speaker in the Chair' is passed round the building verbally by the Police. Members who were not in the Chamber for Prayers may then enter.

Appendix 2

From the Memorandum of the Study of Parliament Group

SELECT COMMITTEES

Valuable as is the work of the Estimates Committee in its scrutiny of balance and economy within individual services (and its value can be assessed by a comparison with the work of the inter-war Estimates Committee) we think that the time has come to increase the membership of the Estimates Committee so that its sub-committees can review the expenditure of the main departments every year and that membership of these sub-committees should be subject to as little change as possible. The Committee would continue on occasion to consider, as at present, problems common to several departments.

The Estimates Committee already has terms of reference wide enough to embrace all aspects of the efficient conduct of administration, as evidenced by examples of its Reports during the Session 1963-4. These included in addition to Supplementary Estimates and Variation in Estimates, topics such as Transport Aircraft, Form of the Estimates of the Defence Department, Treasury Control of Establishments, the Forestry Commission, Services Colleges, Military Expenditure Overseas and the Department of Technical Co-operation. Special Reports relating to Departmental Observations included those on the Home Office, the Administration of the Local Employment Act, 1960, and the Ordnance Survey.

In order to extend the scope of this work we recommend:

(a) that the Estimates Committee should be enlarged to make possible the use of more sub-committees, which would specialize in particular areas so as to cover the whole field of Government vote-borne operations and report on the conduct of administration and on matters necessary for the understanding of policy questions.

(b) Specialist Committees are needed to scrutinize the actions of government in their own fields, to collect, discuss, and report evidence relevant to proceedings in Parliament, whether legislative or other. The main weakness in Parliament's present methods of scrutinizing administration, and indeed of debating policy matters, is the limited ability to obtain the background facts and understanding essential for any detailed criticism of administration or any informed discussion of policy. Specialist committees, working on lines similar to those of the Estimates Committee or Nationalized Industries Committee (itself a fairly recently established specialist committee) could go a long way to remedy this. They would be mainly concerned with administration and would normally seek to avoid matters of policy which are controversial between the major political parties. They could carry out valuable inquiries into matters of direct concern to many ordinary citizens, such as hospital administration, prison rules, training of teachers and agricultural research. Their reports would be fully argued and their evidence would be detailed, but we do not envisage that the deliberations of such committees would be reported or that they should debate publicly.

(c) Specialist Committees of Advice and Scrutiny should eventually cover the whole field of administration.

(d) five such committees might be considered as an initial experiment:

> Scientific Development.
> The Prevention and Punishment of Crime.
> Machinery of National, Regional and Local Government and Administration.
> Housing, Building and Land Use.
> The Social Services.

(e) as new specialist committees are set up, however, the Estimates Committee should devolve its relevant functions to them in their respective spheres.

(f) the proposed specialist committees might eventually at least form the nucleus for the standing committees. We note other suggestions for committees to examine proposals for legislation before bills are drafted. Our specialist committees could perform such a function if desired.

(g) as regards delegated legislation there would again be overlapping membership with the proposed new committee on the merits of statutory instruments. In addition specialist committees would pay particular regard to how these instruments were operating in practice.

(h) the procedures and powers of specialist committees should be those of ordinary select committees. A suggested 'order of reference' is: 'To examine the assumptions on which policy decisions have been made and to report on the implementation of policy in the field of . . .'.

(i) notwithstanding the above proposals for specialist committees, we are of the opinion that the House should make more use of the select committee procedure for ad hoc reports and investigation into matters of current concern, as was the practice in the last century.

(j) Ministers should not be members of specialist committees but could, of course, appear as witnesses before them.

Conclusion

Parliamentary scrutiny of the Executive is fundamental to the whole question of parliamentary reform. The main task of the Government is to govern; the main tasks of Parliament are to sustain the Government and to criticize its policies and actions. We underline the general basis of our approach by the firm assertion that parliamentary control means influence, not direct power, advice, not command, criticism, not obstruction, scrutiny, not initiative, and publicity, not secrecy. We believe that strong government needs

critical opposition; it can benefit from such criticism and stand up
to it. Political control, thus conceived, does not directly hinder
governments; sometimes it can even help them to anticipate trouble.
But to be effective, such control necessitates informed contributions
to deliberation by Members and a fairer balance between Government and Private Member. It follows, we believe, that there must be
a greater degree of specialization by Members and the committees
through which, increasingly, they should work, and that such techniques should be used to obtain more of the relevant facts upon
which any intelligent criticism must be based.

The changes we have suggested do not, in our view, infringe in
any way the principle of ministerial responsibility; they would certainly not involve the oft-cited 'weaknesses and defects' of the French
and American systems which operate in entirely different constitutional and political conditions. In so far as our proposals envisage
more work being taken upstairs in committee, we believe that they
would not replace debate on the floor of the House, but rather give
such debate authoritative depth; they would not infringe but rather
make more real rights of Members of the House of Commons.

Appendix 3

Memorandum submitted by Rt. Hon. F. W. Jowett, M.P.
to the Committee on Procedure, 1931

DEFECT OF PARLIAMENTARY MACHINE

There can be no doubt that the authority and prestige of the House of Commons have been declining in recent years. The cause of this decline must primarily be traced to its unsuitable machinery of procedure, which renders the activities of Opposition parties and private Members largely ineffective except for the purpose of obstruction.

(a) Legislation

Many important Government measures receive no consideration at all, owing chiefly to the existence of a sort of bottle-neck passage at the Committee stage. They are thus effectively obstructed. At the same time, the precedence which the Government's legislative proposals com. and on the Order Paper prevents consideration of the legislative proposals of the Opposition parties, except by consent of the Government. This means in the present Parliament that two parties (Conservative and Liberal), representing 14,000,000 voters, have no opportunity to promote legislation; indeed, one party (the Liberal), representing 5,300,000 voters, has little prospect of being able to do so in the next succeeding Parliament or, possibly, at any time.

(b) Administration

In theory, the House of Commons has the right to control the administration of every public department. But under modern conditions it has been deprived of this right. The public administration of the whole of Great Britain cannot be adequately passed in review and fully considered in twenty days; and a body of 615 members is too unwieldy to control supply effectively. Except on special occasions of personal or political importance, only a few Members are present and even the meagre personnel in attendance is constantly changing. In actual practice, most of the money votes are not offered for consideration at all, but are put to the vote by agreement between the whips or closured under the guillotine, without any consideration whatever.

(c) Committee System

The present committee system is both a fruitful cause of deliberate obstruction, and ineffective for its purpose. The system of discussing details of legislation or administration on the floor of the House is so hopeless that for the most part Members make no pretence of following the proceedings, and show no interest except to hear an especially interesting speech and to vote not for or against the proposal under consideration but for or against the Government then in office.

PROPOSALS FOR REFORM

To restore parliamentary control over the Executive, and to relieve pressure of business and so enable full consideration to be given to the details of legislation, the House of Commons must completely abandon the practice of going into Committee of the Whole House, and pass all its Committee work up to Standing Committees. It is suggested that there should be a Standing Committee responsible for considering matters appropriate to each Ministry, including the Supply Votes for that Ministry. Such a Standing Committee should have the right to question directly permanent officials of the Ministry for which it was responsible, and for this purpose should automatically have the powers in this direction which the House of Commons has extended to the Public Accounts Committee and the Select Committee on Estimates. To guard against obstruction of business, the Chairmen of Standing Committees should automatically be given all the powers of regulating the conduct of debates which are vested in the Speaker.

The Standing Committee on Finance would have duties somewhat wider in range than the others, in that it would also have the duties now performed by the Committee of Ways and Means. Thus it would have the following matters referred to it:

(a) Supply Votes for the Treasury and allied Departments;
(b) Ways and Means resolutions governing the raising of taxation;
(c) Issues out of the Consolidated Fund;
(d) Committee stage of Finance Bills;
(e) Money resolutions in connection with other Bills.

In this way it would have under consideration Treasury policy in its relation both to the budgetary position and to the broader national aspects of financial policy.

The House of Commons would thus be relieved of a mass of specialist and detailed work, and could then concentrate effectively upon broad questions of policy. Legislative proposals would come before it on Second Reading, and again on Report; in the event of objection to details or drafting of a Bill sent to it by a Standing Committee, it should not attempt to alter the actual phraseology of the Bill, but should re-commit the Bill to the Standing Committee accompanied by a series of instructions in the form of resolutions embodying its desires, and it would be the duty of the Committee to amend the Bill accordingly. On the Report stage of Supply Votes it would have an opportunity of discussing the broader issues of administrative policy; and, if such a discussion was desired in the middle of the year, the appropriate Supply Vote could be reported by the Standing Committee concerned, and could then be re-

committed. The broad issues of the raising of revenue and its allocation between different services would fall to be decided as at present
by Ministers in consultation with the Treasury.

In addition to enabling the House of Commons to function more
effectively, it would be possible to reduce the duration of its sittings.
Standing Committees could meet in the mornings, and relatively
short meetings in the afternoons would suffice for the main House.
Alternatively, certain days each week could be fixed days for Committee work, and on other days the House could meet as often as
necessary or advisable to meet.

Appendix 4

Extracts from Fourth Report of the Select Committee on Procedure 1965

Your Committee are convinced that a main purpose of parliamentary reform must be to increase the efficiency of the House of Commons as a debating chamber. At the same time no change should be allowed to supersede the traditional right of the Commons to consider grievances before granting supply nor to absolve them from their duty to examine Government expenditure and administration. In order to achieve this latter purpose Your Committee have come to the conclusion that more information should be made available to Members of the way Government departments carry out their responsibilities, so that, when taking part in major debates on controversial issues, they may be armed with the necessary background of knowledge. This requires that the House should possess a more efficient system of scrutiny of administration. Your Committee are aware that the 'responsibilities' of Government departments are in fact the responsibilities of Ministers. They refer to the departments rather than the Ministers in this Report as a way of distinguishing between responsibility for the 'administrative policy' of day-to-day departmental administration, with which the Report is concerned, and responsibility for policy questions of political significance.

It is to be expected that Members of Parliament will consider that their work would be improved if they were able to become better informed about the work of the executive; and it may also be expected that those who see the situation from the point of view of government will have some reservations in this connection. Your Committee attach importance, therefore, to the evidence of three academic observers of the constitution, the whole tenor of whose submissions was to the effect that the machinery of Parliament has failed to keep pace with the increase in the scope of governmental activity, and that the problem is that of enabling Members 'more effectively to influence, advise, scrutinize and criticize' . . .

In accepting the need to improve the House's sources of information, Your Committee have turned their attention to the Select Committee system as the means of achieving this end. In doing so they have sought to avoid disturbing the relationship of Ministers to Parliament, and also the creation or extension of procedures which might drain away interest from the proceedings of the House as a whole. The object is to provide all Members with the means to carry out their responsibilities, rather than to elevate any Committees of the House to new positions of influence.

The Clerk Assistants' Memorandum makes it clear that the Estimates Committee already provide a wide review of the field of Government administration. All the witnesses who appeared before

Your Committee, however, agreed that greater depth would be given to their Reports if there could be more specialized consideration of particular topics. The head of the Civil Service referred to the 'limitation that the Sub-Committees of the Estimates Committee are of necessity somewhat unfamiliar with the ground they intend to traverse when they begin on their operations', and he contrasted this with the usefulness of the 'experienced' Comptroller and Auditor General in 'suggesting lines of approach to problems' to the Public Accounts Committee. Your Committee consider that specialization under broad subject headings such as 'Social Services', 'Defence and Foreign Affairs', etc., would both increase the value of the work done by the Committee and make it more interesting to Members.

The principal duty of the Estimates Committee is 'to examine such of the estimates presented to this House as may seem fit to the Committee and report how, if at all, the policy implied in those estimates may be carried out more economically. The Committee can thus range over the whole field of ministerial administrative responsibility and have been able, within those terms of reference, to ask the question 'are the managerial arrangements under which expenditure takes place fully effective?' as well as the more limited question of what specific economies might be made. In addition to 'value for money', and the investigation of variations between current and past estimates and the form of the estimates, which the Estimates Committee carry out, there is a need for investigation of the long-term proposals and prospects for expenditure in the various fields (such as the 'forward looks') and an examination of the administrative policy of Government departments, freed from the considerations of economy alone. The Clerk Assistant proposed to Your Committee that the principal order of reference of a revised investigating Committee might be 'to examine how the departments of state carry out their responsibilities', and it appears to Your Committee that such an order of reference would provide a good basis for the type of work they have in mind.

It is not the wish of Your Committee that 'specialist' committees should become involved in matters of political controversy. Many witnesses emphasized the dangers, both for the relations of the House with Ministers, and for the effectiveness of the Committees' work, if the range of investigation got beyond that which could properly be replied to by civil servants.

Your Committee do not pretend that the distinction between what are policy questions and what are not is an easy one to make, and they note the anxieties of the Head of the Civil Service. They do believe, however, that the example of the Nationalized Industries Committee, in producing informative and objective Reports in what is politically a highly sensitive field is one that could profitably be followed by committees specializing in the activities of Government Departments.

In considering the form which specialist committees should take, your Committee have been anxious to retain the experience and method of work of the Estimates Committee. Not only has a useful relationship between that Committee and Government departments been evolved, but the system of operating through sub-committees allows a useful measure of co-ordination to be exercised through Sub-Committee A which would be lacking were independent committees to be set up. On the other hand, your Committee wish to mark the fact that the specialist committees would be expected to carry out wider functions than the present Estimates Committee. They accordingly recommend that a new Select Committee should be developed from the Estimates Committee, which would work through sub-committees each named according to its special subject, such as, for example, 'The Sub-Committee on the Social Services'. In addition to these sub-committees, there would be a steering sub-committee and at least one other sub-committee to consider supplementary estimates and the form of the estimates and carry out investigations 'across the board' of Government expenditure and control. The order of reference of the new Committee would be 'to examine how the departments of state carry out their responsibilities and to consider their Estimates of Expenditure and Reports'.

Your Committee do not recommend at present any large increase in the membership of the new Committee compared with the numbers who serve on the Estimates Committee. They consider that whereas a new interest in the work of the sub-committee might develop from their specialist character, their present investigatory function might be damaged by a sudden large increase in numbers. If the specialist groupings proposed by the Clerk Assistant were adopted, however, an additional sub-committee would need to be appointed.

Your Committee were told in evidence that the power to send for persons, papers and records has proved adequate in the past. They accordingly make no recommendation on this subject, but they wish to emphasize the importance they attach to a close working relationship between the Committee and the departments. In the event of a serious clash, the Government of the day can always use its majority to refuse information to a Committee. Your Committee consider that such a clash can be avoided, without impairing the effectiveness of the proposed Committee. If useful results are to be achieved, however, Your Committee believe that a close liaison between the Committee and the Departments will have to be attained, which may call for day-to-day relationships between officers of the Committee and civil servants. The form of such liaison, however, they believe should be left to the Committee to decide, in the light of experience.

Your Committee recommend that all Select Committees of the House, and their sub-committees, should have authority (subject to the usual permission of the House) to travel abroad if they consider that the nature of their enquiries requires it.

Your Committee's recommendations are as follow:

(i) That a new Select Committee be set up, as a development of the present Estimates Committee, 'to examine how the departments of state carry out their responsibilities and to consider their Estimates of Expenditure and Reports'.

(ii) That the new Committee should function through sub-committees specializing in the various spheres of governmental activity.

(iii) That there should be two clerks supervising the work of the Committee and one full-time clerk to each sub-committee. The Committee should be able to employ specialist assistance.

(iv) That the power of Select Committees to adjourn from place to place should include the power to travel abroad, with the leave of the House, when investigations require it.

Index